Prince Desire dancing with Princess Aurora and the wood nymphs.

Published through the cooperation of VAAP Copyright Agency of the Soviet Union.

Distributed in the UNITED STATES by T.F.H. Publications, Inc., 211 West Sylvania Avenue, Neptune City, NJ 07753; in CANADA to the Book Trade by Macmillan of Canada (A Division of Canada Publishing Corporation), 164 Commander Boulevard, Agincourt, Ontario M1S 3C7; in ENGLAND by T.F.H. Publications Limited, 4 Kier Park, Ascot, Berkshire SL5 7DS; in AUSTRALIA AND THE SOUTH PACIFIC by T.F.H. (Australia) Pty. Ltd., Box 149, Brookvale 2100 N.S.W., Australia; in NEW ZEALAND by Ross Haines & Son, Ltd., 18 Monmouth Street, Grey Lynn, Auckland 2, New Zealand; in SINGAPORE AND MALAYSIA by MPH Distributors (S) Pte., Ltd., 601 Sims Drive, #03/07/21, Singapore 1438; in the PHILIPPINES by Bio-Research, 5 Lippay Street, San Lorenzo Village, Makati Rizal; in SOUTH AFRICA by Multipet Pty. Ltd., 30 Turners Avenue, Durban 4001. Published by T.F.H. Publications, Inc. Manufactured in the United States of America by T.F.H. Publications, Inc.

THE AUTHORIZED BOLSHOI BALLET BOOK OF
SLEEPING BEAUTY

Natalya Bessmertnova as Princess Aurora.

Yuri Grigorovich
&
Victor V. Vanslov

Translated by Yuri S. Shirokov
Photography by Vladimir Pchalkin
Captions to color photographs by Dr. Herbert R. Axelrod

The Bolshoi Hall in Moscow.

THE SLEEPING BEAUTY
A three-act ballet with a Prologue.
Music by Peter I. Tchaikovsky
Libretto by Ivan Vsevolzhsky and Marius Petipa
After Charles Perrault's fairy-tale.

Produced by Marius Petipa in 1890.
Revived in Yuri Grigorovich's version in 1973.

In order to understand the story of *The Sleeping Beauty*, and the meaning of the various dances and scenes, begin reading the captions to the photographs starting on page 81. A synopsis of the ballet is on page 80.

CONTENTS

Yuri Grigorovich.

FOREWORD

The Sleeping Beauty, to the music of Peter Ilyich Tchaikovsky, was the first ballet I ever saw. Its very first scene took my breath away. My young imagination was captivated, so much so that I sat motionless, as if mesmerized, throughout the performance. I lost all touch with reality and lived in a dream world of beauty, chivalry and magic.

That was an unforgettable experience which added much to my desire to dedicate my life to ballet.

As a ballet school pupil I danced in the famous waltz of the corps de ballet in *The Sleeping Beauty* and later, as a member of the celebrated Kirov Ballet of Leningrad, I danced the part of Puss in Boots.

When I became a choreographer, I could not, at first, even dream of staging *The Sleeping Beauty*, although far from everything in its contemporary Leningrad production seemed satisfactory to me.

As my experience grew, however, I felt an increasing attraction to this brilliant ballet and an eager desire to stage its new version.

In my version of 1963, I sought to reveal what was the most valuable in Petipa's choreography and stage the ballet on the principle of continual and integral dance action, in particular, by making the parts of Prince Desire and Fairy Carabosse more meaningful dance parts. Although my efforts were commended as fruitful, in my heart of hearts I felt skeptical about some elements in my choreography.

As time went on, I realized growing with clarity the enormity of the profound message of the ballet. Therefore, a plan to reveal its content more completely and more vividly gradually matured in my mind.

So after a period of ten years I finally produced a version of *The Sleeping Beauty* which satisfied me. The public praised it, too, and it has been a success in many countries of the world.

This book is a story about the making of the ballet, about Tchaikovsky's music and Petipa's choreography, and about different versions of *The Sleeping Beauty*. It also contains a detailed and competent analysis of my own production.

I shall be happy if this book helps the reader to form a better understanding of my version, since I have put into it all the ardor of my heart and all my imagination.

The Sleeping Beauty is among my very favorite ballets to this day.

Yuri Grigorovich

The history of the ballet

I January 17, 1899 — December 28, 1902
Conductor: A. Arends
Choreographer: M. Petipa
Transfer of the ballet from St. Petersburg to
Moscow — A. Gorsky
Designers: K. Waltz (machinery),
A. Geltzer (panorama), I. Savitsky, I. Smirnov,
P. Lebedev, P. Sergeyev
47 performances

II December 19, 1904 — January 26, 1919
Conductor: Ye. Plotnikov
Choreographer: A. Gorsky
Original scenery
71 performances

III May 25, 1924 — June 6, 1934
Conductor: Yu. Faier
Choreographer: A. Gorsky
Revived by V. Tikhomirov
Designer: A. Geltzer
107 performances

IV December 20, 1936 — January 9, 1945
Conductor: Yu. Faier
Choreographers: A. Messerer, A. Chekrygin
Production directed by B. Mordvinov
Designer: I. Rabinovich
71 performances

V April 9, 1952 — February 7, 1958
Conductor: Yu. Faier
Choreographers: A. Messerer, M. Gabovich
Designer: M. Obolensky
Costumes by L. Silich
61 performances

VI December 7, 1963 — May 5, 1971
Conductor: B. Khaikin
Production by M. Petipa
New edition by Yuri Grigorovich
Designer: S. Virsaladze
59 performances

VII May 31, 1973
Conductor: A. Kopylov
Choreographer: M. Petipa
Ballet revived and edited by Yu. Grigorovich
Designer: S. Virsaladze

PETER TCHAIKOVSKY (1840-1893)

INTRODUCTION

The Sleeping Beauty to the music of Tchaikovsky, the greatest of Russian composers, in the choreography of Marius Petipa, who was equally brilliant in his own field, is one of the most spectacular achievements in the history of world ballet.

This is one of Tchaikovsky's most radiant and optimistic creations. Its music is a veritable hymn to life, humaneness, noble and beautiful feelings. In the images of this fairy tale the composer has embodied the idea of the triumph of the forces of life, love and beauty over the dark forces of evil and death.

This composition is remarkable for its emotionality and depth, as well as truly symphonic scope. It is a superlative specimen of Tchaikovsky's reform in the area of ballet music.

This ballet also summed up Petipa's long and persistent quests of new forms of choreographic dramaturgy and methods of symphonic ballet. It was the summit of perfection of his art and a classical model of a large scale production in academic style with rich imagery, varied and elaborate forms of dance.

The Sleeping Beauty has been a regular item in the repertoire of ballet theaters for about a century. It has influenced to a varying extent the music of all the great ballet composers: Alexander Glazunov, Igor Stravinsky, Maurice Ravel, Sergei Prokoviev, Boris Asafiev, Reinhold Glière, and Aram Khachaturian, to mention but a few.

This ballet was a veritable school of artistry for a constellation of great ballerinas whose brilliant skill and creativity have set the guidelines for the progress of the art of dance in the twentieth century. They range from Marina Semenova and Galina Ulanova to Maya Plisetskaya and Natalya Bessmertnova, Margot Fonteyn and Guillen Thesmar.

The Sleeping Beauty has excited the interest of millions of people in the exquisite art of ballet, strengthened their faith in goodness, and given them unforgettable moments of aesthetic pleasure and enjoyment of the beauty and perfection of the wonderful synthesis of music and dance. This ballet is, indeed, one of the world's beloved favorites.

The Sleeping Beauty has a long and eventful stage history which dates back to Petipa's first production. In this history there have been versions which embodied the composer's and the choreographer's conceptions more or less adequately, as well as failures and setbacks, imperfect and rough interpretations.

Yuri Grigorovich's version of *The Sleeping Beauty*, which had its first night at the Bolshoi in 1973, was a milestone in the history of choreographic art. Relying on Petipa's general plan of the choreography and making imaginative use of whatever valuable components of the original production had survived, Grigorovich presented a much more profound, as well as modern interpretation of Tchaikovsky's music in a ballet that was remarkably integral and absolutely perfect in blending the choreography, the music and the stage scenery in an integral whole.

He deepened the original conception of the ballet, developed its dance forms in elaborate detail, and made its message more vivid and meaningful.

This book authentically relates the events that led to the creation of *The Sleeping Beauty*, its music and first presentation on the ballet stage, as well as the story of Grigorovich's production, which is the summit of its theatrical success.

Conductor
Alexander Kopylov

Choreographer
Marius Petipa

Choreographer
Yuri Grigorovich

Designer
Simon Virsaladze

The Birth of The Sleeping Beauty

The idea of composing *The Sleeping Beauty* was suggested to Tchaikovsky by Ivan Vsevolzhsky, Director of the Russian Imperial Theaters between 1881 and 1899. He was a far better educated and many faceted personality than his predecessors in that post. He wrote scenarios for operas and ballets and drew sketches of costumes for the casts. Russian theatrical art and music owe a number of brilliant operas and ballets to his initiative and foresight.

Vsevolzhsky went out of his way to safeguard the theaters under his supervision against a decline and monotonous repertoire and to advance the artistic significance and quality of productions.

He felt great affection for 17th- and 18th-century French culture and dreamt of reviving the magnificent theatrical entertainment of the Royal court of the epoch of French classicism.

It was probably not accidental, therefore, that he chose the fairy-tale *The Beauty of a Dormant Forest* (*La Belle au bois dormant*) by the well-known 17th-century author Charles Perrault (1697). It was not new to the ballet stage. In 1829, the première of a ballet under the same name by the French composer Jean Hérold in Jean Aumer's choreography had been staged at the Paris Opéra and revived at the Drury Lane Theater in London in 1833.

In contrast to the libretto of E. Scribb written in the genre of comedy and adventure, Vsevolzhsky based the scenario only on the first part of Perrault's fairy-tale — from the heroine's birth to her wedding — to bring the libretto closer to its source.

In a letter to Tchaikovsky dated 13 May, 1888, Vsevolzhsky wrote: "I have a plan to write a libretto on the motifs of *La Belle au bois dormant* after Perrault's fairy-tale. I intend to make the mise en scène in the style of Louis XIV.

"One may give free rein to his musical fantasy here and invent melodies in the spirit of Lully, Bach, Rameau, and so on and so forth.... The final act will certainly need a quadrille of all of Perrault's fairy-tales; there must be Puss in Boots, Hop-o'-My-Thumb, Cinderella, Bluebeard, and others."

Tchaikovsky delayed his answer to that letter for a long time. In the meantime, he was musing on the idea of composing a ballet on the subject of *Ondine*, a fairy-tale by Baron de La Motte-Fouqué, in V.A. Zhukovsky's translation in verse, which he admired.

The poor libretto he was offered, however, made him change his mind. Once he had received the completed scenario of *The Sleeping Beauty* from Vsevolzhsky on 22 August, 1888, all his doubts and vacillations evaporated, and in December of the same year he set about composing the music for it with great enthusiasm.

Before that Tchaikovsky had met with Petipa to discuss the general plan and individual scenes of the ballet. Petipa had drawn up and handed over to the composer a detailed plan of his production, which he amended, specified and finalized as Tchaikovsky worked on the music.

It may be relevant to point out here the following two distinctive features of Tchaikovsky's creativity, which were strikingly manifest during his composition of *The Sleeping Beauty*.

One of the most emotional and inspired composers in the history of world music, Tchaikovsky, paradoxically as it may seem at first glance, liked to write music to order. He repeatedly refers to this fact in his letters and diaries; his brother Modest Tchaikovsky, who was the librettist of many of his works, confirms this, too: "He had no fear of orders and deadlines but, on the contrary, drew inspiration from them, so much so that he usually completed his assignment ahead of schedule."

The composer himself admitted in a letter to his publisher Peter Jurgenssen: "I must confess I like to work in a hurry when my music is being expected and I am being spurred on. This has no adverse effect on the quality of my compositions. *The Sleeping Beauty* may well be the best among them, though I composed it in an incredibly short space of time."

Tchaikovsky pointed out that in composing music on request, an external stimulus to creativity, and the need to meet deadlines added to his discipline and organization while detracting nothing from his inspiration.

However, this only holds true of situations where an external incentive agrees with an inner motive, and an order for music was not discrepant with the composer's creative ideas and interests. Tchaikovsky would never agree to work under duress and compose what would not be consistent with his own desire. Whenever a request agreed with his own aspirations, he composed music with skillful ease and enthusiasm.

The Sleeping Beauty is an example in point. Later Tchaikovsky would write in a letter to N.F. von Meck: "The music of this ballet will be one of my best compositions. The subject is so poetic and noble and very good for the music; I am fascinated with it and it lends my work warmth of feeling and inspiration, indispensable for the good merits of any composition."

Petipa's stiff demands were not onerous to Tchaikovsky. Seeking to create music that would be profound in meaning, vivid in imagery, expressive dramatically and well-developed symphonically, he seemed to visualize the future ballet as a fusion of music with choreography and stage action.

For his part, Petipa, approaching the subject from the opposite side, as it were, sought to achieve the unity of the choreography and the music and in composing dances and dance scenes imagined the music suitably expressive of his ideas. Therefore, he discussed with Tchaikovsky not only the general plan of the action, individual dance scenes and mise en scènes, but also told him sometimes of the character of music he desired for the ballet, its rhythm and meter, and even requested a definite number of bars for every choreographic number.

Here are a few examples from Petipa's musical and choreographic plan.

"The King, Queen and four Princes appear on the palace terrace. The music is in characteristic noble style. Eight bars for the entrance to the terrace. Four bars for the question and four bars for the answer; this repeats four times. Broad 2/4's. For instance:— Question: 'Where are you taking these women?' Answer: 'To jail.' Question: 'What wrong has been done by these women?' Four bars. Catalabutte presents incriminating evidence. Thirty-two to forty-eight bars. The King is frightened and angry: 'Let them be punished as they deserve.' Twenty-four bars of vigorous music." (2nd scene, 1st act).

"Princess Aurora suddenly catches sight of an old woman, who is beating time 2/4 with her spindle and begins to move at a rhythm of 3/4, to very merry and melodious music, swinging the spindle in time. When the music is changed to 3/4, Aurora snatches the spindle out of her hands and raises it aloft like a scepter. Thirty-two bars. All delight in the music. Twenty-four bars of the waltz. All of a sudden (pause), she feels pain. Her finger is bleeding. Eight bars at 4/4 broad movement." (ibid)

Petipa's entire plan is drawn up in this spirit. Tchaikovsky studied it very carefully and reckoned with it in composing the music. It is true, rather than comply with Petipa's requirements unquestioningly, Tchaikovsky sometimes offered him his own suggestions which Petipa readily accepted.

Composers had collaborated with ballet-masters before but never as closely and fruitfully as Tchaikovsky and Petipa did. Their mutual understanding was complete, because they pusued a common goal: to deepen the message and enrich the imagery of ballet and symphonize both the music and the choreography. There is evidence, it is true, that Petipa occasionally found it difficult to adapt to Tchaikovsky's innovative ideas, but eventually there was an integrated whole based on complete accord.

Their work proceeded at a brisk pace and their enthusiasm never waned, sustaining their creativity at its best. The Prologue and the First Act were completed in December 1888. On January 23, 1889, Tchaikovsky played almost the whole of the Second Act for Vsevolzhsky and Petipa. During the next spring and summer he composed the fifth scene. There was no respite, even during his travel abroad. On May 22, 1889, Tchaikovsky reported in a letter: "I am finishing the sketches of the final act of the ballet, and I will get down to instrumentation about June 1. There will be a mountain of work. When I was in St. Petersburg, I saw mock-ups of stage scenery and drawings of costumes at the office of the Director of the Imperial Theaters. It will be a ballet with nothing on record comparable to it in splendor."

In June 1889, Tchaikovsky completed composing the music and set about instrumentation. Finally, he announced in a letter of August 16: "I deserve congratulations: today I have completed the enormous score of *The Sleeping Beauty*, and now I feel I have moved mountains."

That was titanic work, indeed. Tchaikovsky had composed the biggest of his ballets in nine months, which was an all-time record. He had created it without catching his breath, so to say, in one sustained effort. It indisputably contributed to the symphonic unity and integrity, emotionality and inspiration of his music.

The Sleeping Beauty had its first night on the Marinsky stage on January 3, 1890. The cast consisted of the finest dancers of the time. The central part of Princess Aurora was danced by Carlotta Brianza, an Italian ballerina trained by the famous Carlo Blasis. She had worked in Russia since 1887. Her youth, beauty and superb virtuosity made her an idol of the ballet-going public.

The decor was designed by a few artists, which was the custom at the time unlike today's practice of employing one designer. The best-known among them were M.I. Bocharov, K.M. Ivanov, and M.A. Shishkov.

The costumes were made to the sketches of I.A. Vsevolzhsky himself. The stage scenery was luxuriant and picturesque, reflecting Vsevolzhsky's flair for French mythology, as the composer N.A. Rimsky-Korsakov said after seeing the première. Evidently, not all of this stylization was consistent with refined taste. One should bear in mind, however, that many episodes in Tchaikovsky's music are remarkable for their orchestral power, intricate texture, and magnificence. A modest, deliberately simplified and laconic scenery would have been inappropriate for the music of *The Sleeping Beauty*.

The conductor at the première was R.E. Drigo, who had held the post of Kapellmeister (musical director) of the Marinsky ballet since 1886. A subtle connoisseur of ballet and a ballet composer himself, Drigo followed the tradition of Cesare Pugni and Ludwig Minkus.

Drigo would later form a profound understanding of Tchaikovsky's music and greatly contribute to the success of his *Swan Lake*. At the time of the première of *The Sleeping Beauty*, however, he had not yet fully appreciated the significance of Tchaikovsky's reform in the genre of ballet music. He could have done more to bring the message of Tchaikovsky's music to the listeners, who failed to appreciate it immediately.

In their comments on the première critics were, as a rule, skeptical and, as far as the music was concerned, some of them took a frankly negative stand. Here is an example in point: "Messrs. balletomanes alleged after the première that this music with 'symphonic combinations' was no good for ballet, that the rhythm was at places not clear enough, and so on. Some special criticisms levied at the composer were perhaps well-grounded."

Today we are amused to read the reproaches of Tchaikovsky for his music being too serious and symphonic, unmelodious and unfit for dance. It will be recalled, however, that similar complaints were addressed to other innovative composers: Igor Stravinsky, Sergei Prokofiev, and Rodion Shchedrin, to mention but a few.

Evidently, there is a general law that governs the maturation of critical opinion; since Tchaikovsky's day ballet music has been continually enriched with achievements of modern symphonic music, which were at times at variance with the traditional requirement of fitness for dance, the habitual dance patterns, and were not duly appreciated by the music critics immediately.

The only critic of the time to have displayed perspicacity in his assessment of the première was Hermann Laroche. In an article on *The Sleeping Beauty* he linked its music with the Glinka tradition, traced it to its native Russian sources, and described it as one of Tchaikovsky's greatest compositions.

Despite the cool attitude of the press, *The Sleeping Beauty* made quite a hit with the ballet-going public. The house was packed to capacity at every performance. This has been in evidence from the première to the present day. Later, critics would also revise their attitude to the ballet. Tchaikovsky made the following remark after reading the first press reviews of the new production: "Of two evils — discontent of the public or discontent of the press — I certainly choose the latter."

Whatever difference there was between the opinions of the press and the public immediately after the première, it was not long before *The Sleeping Beauty* was recognized by all as one of Tchaikovsky's finest creations.

Léo Delibes.

Tchaikovsky's Music

Peter Ilyich Tchaikovsky (1840-1893) composed *The Sleeping Beauty* in the period when his art was most popular. He was a mature composer with a long record of experience, a celebrated author of four symphonies, a few operas, including *Eugene Onegin*, which was a steady item in the theatrical repertoire, many symphonic and chamber works, and, finally, the ballet *Swan Lake*. The Fifth Symphony and the opera *The Sorceress* which he composed at about the same time have much in common with *The Sleeping Beauty* in their musical dramaturgy and the imagery of the music.

In fact, from the early period of his career as a composer Tchaikovsky had displayed an invariable interest in the dance genres and used them broadly in his symphonic, operatic and chamber works, developing the traditions laid down by Mikhail I. Glinka, whom he revered.

Suffice it to recall the dances in his operas, the folk dance and ball dances in *Eugene Onegin*, the dances of the Gypsies, clowns and dwarfs in *The Maid of Orlèans*, the Ukrainian "hopak" dance in *Mazepa*, the Ukrainian and Russian folk dances in *The Little Shoes* (Tscherevichki) and the dance of buffoons in *The Sorceress*.

Tchaikovsky admired the art of ballet and felt respect for it in contrast to the current opinion of ballet as a trivial and superficial musical genre of secondary importance. When Sergei Taneyev, his favorite pupil, who was already a mature composer at the time, complained that in every movement of Tchaikovsky's Fourth Symphony "there is something reminiscent of ballet music" the latter said: "I fail to see why the term ' ballet music ' should imply something reprehensible. Indeed, ballet music is not always bad; there is good ballet music, too. Take, for instance, *Sylvia* by Léo Delibes."

Sylvia merits special attention in this context. Tchaikovsky saw this ballet in 1877 and was literally enchanted by it. He wrote in a letter: "This is a genuine masterpiece of art. The composer is a Frenchman, Léo Delibes . . . Such elegance, such a wealth of melodies and rhythms, such excellent instrumentation have never been witnessed in ballet . . . I was completely fascinated!"

In another letter he wrote: "I have listened to the ballet *Sylvia* by Léo Delibes; 'listened' is the right word, because this is the first ballet in which the music constitutes the main and only interest. What charm, what refinement, what a wealth of melody, rhythm and harmony!"

Tchaikovsky's delighted comments on *Sylvia*, however, give no reason to presume that he liked any ballet music. In his letters about his travels abroad he mentions several ballets, such as *Excelsior, Trilbi*, and some others he disliked so intensely that he was unable to watch them to the end. This is hardly surprising as at that time ballet in Europe and partly, in Russia, fell into decay.

The hey day of romantic ballet had already passed, but a revival was yet to come. Ballet was degenerating and losing its great ideas; it was turning into shallow and garish entertainment, a variety show catering to the vulgar tastes.

In the 1850's through 1880's numerous ballets by Cesare Pugni, Ludwig Minkus, and Julius Herber were produced on the Russian ballet stage. Their music was devoid of any profound message. These composers pursued no far-reaching imaginative in-depth description of the characters or the situations of events. Quadrilles, polkas, marches, and gallops of identical types were adapted to a diversity of subjects. Stereotyped patterns, clichés and humdrum monotony were often so overwhelming that no lifelike imagery had a chance to survive on stage.

In the literature on Tchaikovsky, his ballet music is invariably opposed to the music of his predecessors for its profound content, vivid images, forceful concreteness, and symphonic character. This is correct, of course.

It should also be remembered, however, that the art of his predecessors had left an imprint on the development of ballet music. Some of their contributions were quite valuable. This refers in the first place to the links of ballet music with genre melodies of everyday life and at times with folk dance, and second, the amazing appropriateness of their music for dance, so that the music lends greater vividness to dance, which in turn adds to listening pleasure.

It should be stressed that not only did Tchaikovsky discard the threadbare clichés of the popular composers of his time, but he also assimilated, further developed and added profundity to some of their valuable ideas of composition.

His innovative ideas in the genre of ballet music were, in fact, a revolutionary reform, which advanced ballet to a higher level of artistry. The music of his ballets not only provides an accompaniment for dance but also paints the characters of the *dramatis personae*, determines situations and the atmosphere of events, and carries the message of great ideals.

Tchaikovsky enriched the art of ballet with the finest achievements of symphonic music of his time and pioneered the profound musical dramaturgy of a ballet performance. "A ballet is a symphony of its own kind," he once remarked.

While expressing delicate and profound emotions and revealing the moral fiber of the action, Tchaikovsky's music retains its fitness for dance, which is a quality indispensable for presenting a rich and sophisticated choreography on the stage. As the music critic Hermann Laroche, who was Tchaikovsky's contemporary, pointed out in his time, "His music is very good for ballet, and it is just as good and interesting for a serious musician."

All these features of Tchaikovsky's ballet music were vividly manifest already in his first ballet *Swan Lake* composed in 1876, and *The Sleeping Beauty* brought them into more salient relief. Tchaikovsky himself felt satisfied with the ballet, which he expressed in this comment: "*The Sleeping Beauty* may be the best of all my compositions." Indeed, his artistic creed is conveyed in its message with great inspiration and sincerity.

The Sleeping Beauty opens with a musical prelude which portrays the main conflict of images through a conflict between two sharply contrastive musical themes. These are the leitmotifs of the forces of good and evil locked in an eternal contest. Since the dawn of time the forces of evil are personified by Fairy Carabosse, an ugly witch obsessed with a malicious idea to plunge the world into darkness for eternity; and the forces of good, by the Fairy Lilac who bestows on human beings the blessings of spring, beauty, youth and happiness.

The theme of Fairy Carabosse played by the full orchestra erupts like a volcano of spite and fury disgorged by the wicked old witch seeking to destroy the young and beautiful Princess Aurora. The evil fairy has no emotions except her hatred of all living things, and her jealousy of human beings enjoying themselves at a festival drives her to frenzy.

Example 1. The theme of Fairy Carabosse *Allegro vivo*

23

The recitative character, ruptured fabric, convulsive twists and grotesquery of this theme is opposed by the smoothly flowing, gentle and dreamy theme of the Fairy Lilac, whose melody played by an hautboy on the tremulous background of the strings is a beautiful lyrical song.

Example 2. The theme of The Lilac Fairy *Andantino Dolce espressivo*

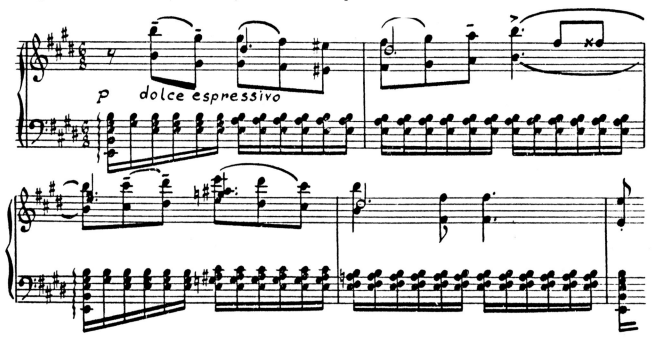

These themes come into a vehement collision not only in the prelude but also throughout the composition. Tchaikovsky would later develop a similar conflict in the introduction to *The Queen of Spades*, where the demoniac theme of the three cards is opposed by the melodious and beautiful theme of love.

The theme of Fairy Carabosse often makes a violent intrusion into the serene flow of the music, for instance, in the Prologue, similar to the themes of destiny in Tchaikovsky's Fourth and Fifth Symphonies. However, it is invariably forced to retreat by the theme of the Lilac Fairy, which symbolizes the triumph of good over evil.

These musical images are profoundly generalized in character. They present the two fairies as eternal antagonists and express the primary conflict of being, the struggle between light and darkness, between the life-giving forces of creation and beauty and the deadly forces of destruction and evil.

The struggle between the radiant forces of life and the dark forces of death in the ballet parallels its heroes' quests for happiness. The image of Princess Aurora has the broadest representation in the music and is central to the drama. Already in the Prologue, the large scene of fairies bringing gifts to her cradle means, in effect, an indirect description of the heroine's character, because each of the fairies bestows her own qualities on the baby girl: tenderness, simple-heartedness, cheerfulness, vigor, and other good attributes which are expressed primarily in the music.

This music is amazingly varied in character, combining each variation based on a very clear-cut and vivid rhythmic pattern of dance with the symphonic continuity of development and the integrity of form which have a common culmination.

There is another important musical and dramaturgical distinction typical of both Tchaikovsky and Petipa in this scene. This is a collection of fragmented episodes of the plot in an integral and complete large form. In the case under review this form is *pas de six* consisting of *entrée* (No. 2, scene of dances), *adagio* (No. 3, prelude), six variations, and a general coda.

This form integrates, in effect, two different numbers in a common musical and, as we shall see later, choreographic development. In this way a complete large scene — from the entrée of the fairies to the finale — is formed. Such enlargement of musical and choreographic forms united by continuous common development is one of the manifestations of Tchaikovsky's symphonic principles in ballet music.

But let us go back to Princess Aurora. Her image is further developed in similar large musical and choreographic scenes — *adagio*, which are the key points in the musical dramaturgy of the ballet. In the First Act this is the scene of Princess Aurora with the four cavaliers asking for her hand. The magnificent and solemn music of this *adagio* with its forceful life-asserting motifs sounds like a radiant hymn to happiness.

Example 3. *Adagio maestoso*

The listener is impressed by the unusual emotional intensity of this and subsequent *adagios* of *The Sleeping Beauty*, which were unusually the most insipid episodes in the old ballets, since the absence of fast, emphatic rhythms exposed, as it were, the languor of melody and harmony. In Tchaikovsky's music, however, the lyrical scenes are unusually meaningful, sincere and beautiful. They reveal the characters' inner world with utmost clarity. The dynamic growth of a few waves of powerful sounds in this *adagio* is yet another method Tchaikovsky used to symphonize ballet music, just as with the inclusion of *adagio* in a larger musical form, *pas d'action*.

Odette, the heroine of Tchaikovsky's first ballet *Swan Lake* was primarily a suffering maiden. Her main musical theme is full of gentle sadness and elegiac melancholy. The heroine of *The Sleeping Beauty*, however, has the name of the goddess of the dawn and is portrayed in lucid, cheerful, hymnic colors almost throughout the ballet. This description is disturbed only at one point where Princess Aurora wounds her finger on the witch's spindle and its lethal poison causes her feverish anxiety. Her swift *danse vertige* in the finale of the First Act expresses her growing restlessness and alarm.

Example 4. *Allegro vivo*

Further on, when Princess Aurora faints away and sinks to the floor lifeless, the cellos play the tragic melody of sobs and grief, which is followed by the furious mockery and sinister laughter of Fairy Carabosse. These sorrowful and demoniac episodes, however, are soon ended by the entry of the lucid and gentle melody of the Lilac Fairy, who saves Princess Aurora from death by putting her to everlasting sleep.

Symphonic ballet music is also heard in the next *adagio* of Princess Aurora in the Second Act, where she appears among the Nereids as a phantom summoned up by the Lilac Fairy to awaken love and vigor in Prince Desire who is destined to rescue Princess Aurora from the spell of the evil magic of Fairy Carabosse.

The broad and lucid melody flowing from the cellos, which is reminiscent of a theme in the slow movement of Tchaikovsky's Fifth Symphony, conveys the motif of Aurora and Desire's love union, while Aurora's playful and graceful variation adds a new trait of innocent coquetry to her image.

The mode of a musical variation on a theme in its dynamic symphonic development was audible in the preceding *adagio*. Here it is more distinct: Princess Aurora's dance variation is a musical variation of her dance duet with Prince Desire.

Example 5. *Andante cantabile Molto espressivo.*

Example 6. *Allegro*

This is continued symphonic development of the music.

In the Third Act Princess Aurora and Prince Desire dance a long duet, which may be described as a song of triumphant love. It includes a majestic and ornate *adagio*, the impassioned variation of Prince Desire and the playful and graceful variation of Princess Aurora, as well as a jubilant coda. This virtuoso duet full of bravura and majesty glorifies the mutual devotion and self-sacrifice of the heroes, the triumph of love, goodness and happiness.

The image of Prince Desire in the music is less developed than the image of Princess Aurora. The Prince does not appear on stage before the Second Act, and his musical image is revealed primarily in his duets with Princess Aurora, in the love that unites them.

At the same time, his musical image goes through some stages of development. At first, the hero seems to mingle with his retinue in the scenes of the picnic and the hunt. Fairy Lilac stirs his romantic emotions, unveils what is unknown to him, and lures him to a mysterious distant land where his faithfulness and self-sacrifice will deliver a beautiful princess from the spell of evil magic. The virile lyricism of his first *adagio* with Princess Aurora is full of charm and beauty. In the final act the solemn, triumphant and heroic motifs complete his image.

Genre scenes and scenes of nature hold a conspicuous place in the ballet. Moments of intensive dramatic action expressing the main conflict alternate with characteristic episodes depicting the surroundings but co-ordinated with the main events. These are the scenes of the Palace with the majestic procession of the courtiers and the funny pranks of Cattalabutte in the Prologue, the scene of the knitting maidens, and the waltz in the First Act with its gentle, undulating and slow melody, the contrastive suite of genre dances in the scene of the picnic in the Second Act, the sharp character dances of "fairy-tales" and the different variations of "gems" at the heroes' wedding in the Third Act.

Finally, the ballet includes the full-scale symphonic scenes "Panorama", "Entr'acte", and "The Dormant Kingdom." They are partly intended for a visual effect, but their main dramaturgical function is different. This is a generalized musical narrative of the beauty of the world, the joy of love, nature and the awakening of the enchanted kingdom to a new life. They intensify and deepen the development of the main theme and are perceived as a musical story of the beauty of life.

Composing *The Sleeping Beauty*, Tchaikovsky did not reject or destroy the external forms of ballet music which had become a matter of course in his time. Like his other ballets, *The Sleeping Beauty* has a numbered structure. Tchaikovsky followed the guidelines set by the time-honored types of musical numbers in ballet: *pas de deux, pas d'action*, a solo variation, a mass dance, a dance scene. He adapted his music to the distinctions of numbers based on classical and character dance, obviously with Petipa's assistance. For their rhythmic "relief" and their "suggestion" of movements the patterns of his dance melodies can vie with the most colorful and effective episodes in the ballets of Minkus and Pugni.

At the same time, Tchaikovsky was the greatest innovator in the art of ballet. His innovation was inseparably linked with tradition, developing, enriching and deepening it.

Tchaikovsky's reform in the art of ballet was a revision of the quality and role of the music in choreography. In his ballets music was elevated to profound and imaginative characterization of the characters and action. Formerly disconnected and independent numbers were blended in a symphonic whole, integrating individual numbers within the limits of a scene or act and expressing the dramatic action. For the first time in the history of ballet it relied on what is known as *musical dramaturgy*, that is, an integral expression of the idea and conception of the work based on a musical description of the characters and dramatic conflict.

This entailed *symphonization* of ballet music, its enrichment with the full variety of means of expression characteristic of the superior achievements of symphonic music. Tchaikovsky's music does not *accompany* the plot and dance but *determines* them; it does not *illustrate* the action but *influences* its development; it does not *supplement* the content of a performance but makes its *foundation*. Sometimes, the music penetrates even the structure of the action, lending it features of musical forms.

All these innovative elements have enabled choreography to cope successfully with significant tasks in expressing the artistic content, which has placed ballet on a par with the finest achievements of other arts. Petipa was Tchaikovsky's like-minded comrade and ally, however hard it might have been at times for him to adapt to the composer's unorthodox concepts, and eventually created a new style of choreography largely congenial with his music.

That was what laid the groundwork for the integral musical and choreographic dramaturgy of *The Sleeping Beauty*. We shall return to it later. Let us now take a look at Petipa's work on the ballet.

Petipa's Choreography

Marius Petipa (1818-1910) was a French dancer and ballet master, who settled in Russia in 1847. Here he found a second home and became Russia's greatest choreographer. His contributions to the development of Russian and world ballet were enormous. He had been trained as a dancer by his father and Vestris and later taught the art of dance himself. Petipa staged ballets of other ballet masters in Russia. In 1862 he was appointed a full-time ballet master, and between 1869 and 1903 he was chief ballet master of the St. Petersburg ballet company.

Petipa staged more than sixty ballets, but far from all of them were successful. In his finest ballets, however, he displayed an unusual wealth of choreographic fantasy, achieved full harmony of the choreographic ensemble, and developed solo parts to virtuoso perfection.

Long before his first meeting with Tchaikovsky, the architectonics of some dance episodes in Petipa's ballets was similar to the structural forms of music, while the system of means of expression followed the principles of musical imagery. In other words, Petipa had been steadily advancing towards symphonization of choreography, not infrequently relying on music absolutely devoid of symphonic qualities.

His most significant productions before his meeting with Tchaikovsky were his own versions of the ballets *La Sylphide*, *Giselle*, *Le Corsaire*, *The Maid of the Danube*, *Coppelia*, and *Esmeralda*, as well as his own ballets *King Candavle* and *La Fille du Pharaoh* by Cesare Pugni, *Don Quixote* and *La Bayadère* by Ludwig Minkus.

Petipa's art had grown out of romantic ballet, whose principles were further developed in his productions, and much of what he had planned before was now reinforced and acquired new and perfect forms of artistic expression.

Petipa is sometimes described as a classic of academic choreographic style. There is a reason behind such a description. It should be borne in mind, however, that his academic style was emphasized precisely in romantic ballet whose image motifs have an essential part to play in any of his works.

A mature composer and a mature choreographer joined forces in creating *The Sleeping Beauty*. Tchaikovsky composed the music in accordance with Petipa's plan, and the latter composed the choreography following Tchaikovsky's musical guidelines. Petipa's inborn musicality was thrown into salient relief by this complete fusion of music and dance, which had rarely been achieved in earlier ballets. Let us examine consecutively Petipa's detailed plan of the choreography of *The Sleeping Beauty*.

Prologue. No. 1. March. There are three episodes here: the entrée of the courtiers, Cattalabutte's frolics, and the entrée of the royal couple. The music is in march style and majestic, with a fanfare of the trumpets for the King's entrée. It is composed in the form of a *rondo* where both episodes (restless and anxious cis-moll and tranquil and gentle fis-moll) are assigned to Cattalabutte. The choreography is based on a pantomime procession with Cattalabutte's mimic play.

No. 2. A dance scene devoted to the entrée of the fairies. The music here is warm and poetic. The entrée of the fairies at a hovering dance step contrasts with the somewhat staid procession of courtiers that preceded it. The next half of this scene is a graceful waltz with the presentation of gifts to the fairies. As is said in Petipa's accompanying remark, "The pages and maidens form picturesque groups and dance" The entire second number is, in effect, an extended entrée for the next number.

No. 3. *Pas de six*. The music of the *adagio*, in which the fairies address the newly-born Aurora, is reminiscent of a lullaby. The variations that follow convey prophecies and good wishes to the royal infant. The fairies seem to be conferring their finest character traits upon her. In the *adagio* they all dance together and then each of them performs her distinctive "portrait" variation.

Fairy Candide. The music is based on a motif of soft, soothing movements. The dancer daintily minces on points, making wavy motions with her arms. Her dance reminds one of a beautiful flower swaying slightly on its slender stalk.

Fairy Fleur de Farine. The music of this lively dance is reminiscent of a tarantella. The fairy makes short and sharp movements, her leg circling as though whipping the air (rond de jambe), while her arms are swiftly spread above her head.

Fairy Miettes qui Tombert (strewing bread crumbs). She dances on points all the time, her movements following the *staccato* style of the music. Her arms seem to be weaving a fanciful pattern, now scattering invisible crumbs, now shaking off drops of dew or playing gaily in an intricate dance pattern. She reminds one of a mischievous teenager.

Fairy Canari qui Chante (singing canary). The music is lively and graceful, in a high register, and is accompanied by the jingling of bells and the roulades of a flute. It is like a short scherzo. The dance is based on mincing steps and point technique. The dancer cups her hands at her mouth as though playing a pipe or spreads her arms like wings or folds and hides them behind her back. In the meantime she swiftly runs across the stage, imitating the flight of a bird.

Fairy Violent. The music is based on quick and vigorous movement in galloping style with sharp rhythmic accents. Her dance is swift and forceful. Her arms cut through the air like lightning or are thrown forward in turn with the index finger extended as though giving an order.

The final variations of the Lilac Fairy is a waltz based on a smoothly flowing and broad melody. The fairy seems to be radiating light and warmth, suffusing the baby princess.

Petipa's choreography of this waltz has not survived to date. When reviving the ballet in Leningrad in 1922, Fedor Lopukhov composed this variation of the Lilac Fairy anew, and it was such a spectacular success that it has since become part and parcel of the canonized choreography of *The Sleeping Beauty*. This choreography is indistinguishable from Petipa's in style. It is based on broad and soft beautiful movements and creates the image of regal majesty of the leading fairy, as well as her open-heartedness and generosity.

The music of the *pas de six* coda infects everybody with its merry motif and is the symphonic culmination of the number. All the fairies dance here as though to remind the audience of the variations presenting their "portraits."

No. 4. The Finale. It is wholly devoted to Fairy Carabosse and ends in the Lilac Fairy's victory over her. The entrée of Fairy Carabosse is preceded by an anxious and excited musical introduction based on sequential increases in an impulsive melody when a page announces Fairy Carabosse's arrival. Further on, the entire episode involving Fairy Carabosse is a symphonic development of her grotesque theme.

Another musical theme appears only at the moment of telling Aurora's fortune. All the rabid bacchanalia of the spiteful witch with her retinue of rats and monsters, however, is swept away by the quiet and confident introduction to the theme of the Lilac Fairy. Fairy Carabosse, seized with impotent fury, is forced to retreat, and the theme of the Lilac Fairy sounds like a song praising the triumph of life.

Petipa choreographed the part of Fairy Carabosse as a pantomime part performed by a male dancer. This imparted energy and forcefulness to the dance, emphasizing the malice and fury of the witch. For all the grotesquery of the music devoted to Fairy Carabosse, its fantastic angular rhythms offer the possibility of including dance components which were not used by Petipa. The prediction of Aurora's fortune was expressed by symbolic gestures devoid of any dramatic elements. The final episode in the finale of the prologue was presented in pantomime mise-en-scènes.

The first act. **No. 5.** A scene of a public gathering. The lively, cheerful music seems to present a visual scene of a large crowd expecting to celebrate a festive occasion. Some women are gossiping with a secretive look on their faces, others are busy with their knitting work. Cattalabutte finds them using sharp needles forbidden in the kingdom. He is angered by this breach of the law and intends to take the culprits to jail. However, the King and Queen make their appearance right at this moment, and the frightened women plead for mercy. The royal couple pardon them. A waltz begins.

Despite this profusion of illustrative details, and the frequent changes in the rhythm and fabric of the music, it is remarkable for its great symphonic integrity. The number does not come to a conclusion but directly changes into an introduction to a waltz. This is yet another method for symphonizing the music of the ballet by obliterating sharp boundaries between individual numbers. At the same time, this method has dramatic significance: at the time when the King is hesitant before granting his pardon, the orchestra sustains an unstable harmony. When the King shows his mercy to the despairing knitters, this unstable harmony resolves into a sigh of relief and smiles, and an introduction to a waltz begins.

Example 7. The King hesitates. He grants pardon.

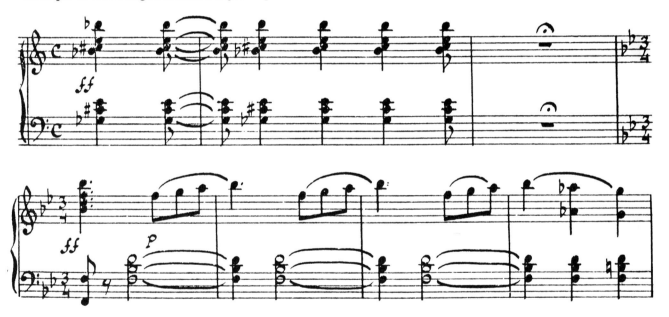

Petipa based all this scene on pantomime. The waltz that follows strikingly contrasts with it, completing the preceding scene and consummating all earlier events.

No. 6. In Tchaikovsky's ballets waltzes are lyrical poems of their own kind. This is equally true of *Swan Lake* and *The Nutcracker*. In *The Sleeping Beauty* this fluent and melodious waltz of long duration and wide sonority should not be described as merely a divertissement episode. It is true, it provides the background for events rather than depicts them. This, however, is the background of the world of Princess Aurora, the theme of happiness reigning supreme in this world and a triumph of poetry. However slight the motive for its emergence may be in the plot, its general significance for the imagery of the ballet is very great indeed. Depicting the world of Princess Aurora, it seems to be indirectly reflecting her image. Praising the harmony and happiness of life, this waltz conveys the fundamental message of the ballet.

The waltz is performed by thirty-two pairs of male and female dancers and children, who dance with garlands and baskets of flowers in their hands. The dance spreads over the stage in undulating resilient waves, their ebb and flow steadily covering more and more ground. The dance is subordinated to a strict symmetry of diverging and converging lines of dancers, crossing each other and forming large and small circles. The fluent and unhurried melody is reflected, as it were, in the combinations of rising and falling figures of the corps de ballet.

It is amazing to see how expertly this waltz and many other masterpieces of dance in Petipa's choreography are based on a small number of simple movements. He relies mainly on *pas de basque, balloñe, balancé* and *pas de bourée*. They are so intricately combined, varied and repeated, however, that they eventually form rich dance compositions of impressive beauty and musicality. Musicality is their chief merit, because in response to the lasting, deliberately simple and rhythmically swaying melody of the waltz Petipa created an equally lasting and simple but compositionally rich "choreographic melody."

Neither soloists, nor coryphées take part in dancing the waltz. It is performed by the corps de ballet alone. Its arrangement and re-arrangement, however, are distinguished by an intricate dance polyphony, a wealth of compositional patterns, an alternation of "unissons" and "imitations," very relevant musical terms here, variations in the thickness of the dancing crowd, an ebb and flow in its movement, and elaboration of the theme and dance motifs. This is a veritable symphony in dance fully consistent with the symphonic scope and rich fabric of Tchaikovsky's music.

Petipa carefully planned the composition of the waltz, sketching many episodes in his drawings. As a result, he created an unsurpassed chef-d'oeuvre, which would be repeatedly revised in later productions, but all efforts to make it more beautiful would prove futile.

Marius Petipa's sketches of the waltz in the First Act of *The Sleeping Beauty*.

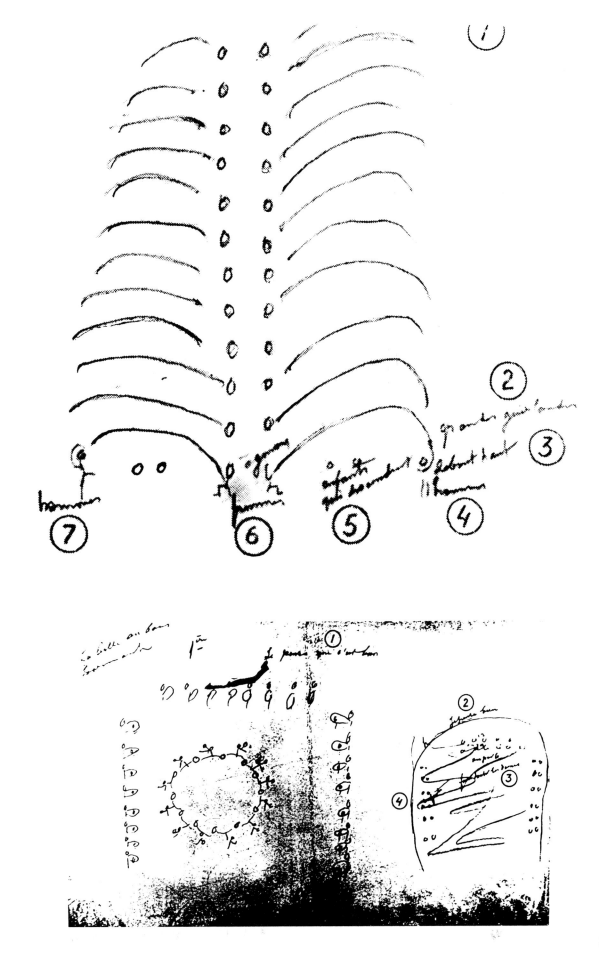

Après la 4e figure ils vont se placer
ainsi en dansant pour seront préparer
le dernier groupes

hant

de présent
les groupes
attendant se
le groupes

moitié de côté

le dire finir le pas en terre au ... les ...
... en valsant

... resté

8 mesures.
8 avec oligarchies de ...
8 mesures.
4 ? ... en changent ... les
4 ? ... de ...
14 mesures.
4 mesures avant de partir en
valsant

10   10+
9   9+
8   8+
7   7+
6   6+
5   5+
4   4+
3   3+
2   2+
1   1+

où je suis resté

Ils font
présent le passe du commencement pour
arriver; les hommes à ... faisant le dernier
les femmes ... pas de garde devant

o x x o o x o x o x o x   x o x o x o x o
o x x o
o x x o
o x x o
o x x o

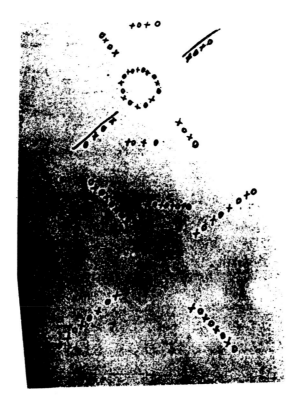

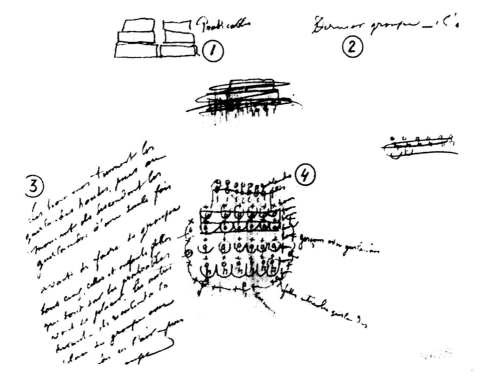

No. 7. A scene. The entrée of the main heroine is preceded by the entrée of the pages and the Maids of Honor, as well as the four Princes who will ask for her hand. The entrée of the ballerina is thoroughly prepared and surrounded with ceremony. Light abrupt sounds as though imitating the rhythm of quick, impatient footsteps come from the orchestra.

Example 8. *Allegro guisto*

Princess Aurora runs down the staircase and abandons herself to joyful playing. Her quick, mincing steps and runs express her cheerfulness and vigor. They change into impetuous spinning movements expressing her delight. The radiant image of Princess Aurora is presented in outline, and it will be further developed in her solemn *adagio* with four cavaliers.

No. 8. *Pas d'action.* This form of dance could also be called *grand pas*. The music of the *adagio* with four cavaliers has been described above. In this scene Princess Aurora seems indifferent to her admirers, but at the same time she is eager to excite their passion.

In the dance she alternately goes from one cavalier to another. Her partners at first support her arm, then offer her their hands to lean upon during her circling motion, and touch her waist in dance. The so-called "upper" supports are completely absent here. The Princes are vying with each other for Princess Aurora's favor, but she is indifferent to all of them and her answers are cool and curt dismissals.

In the *adagio* composition diagonal patterns prevail, which contrast with the preceding waltz of straight lines and frontal arrangements, squares and circles.

The choreography here is beautiful, imaginative and profoundly meaningful. However, it is not fully consistent with the power of the music, its culminations, luxurious fabric and the brilliance of the solo trumpet. Therefore, in later productions choreographers attempted, often without success, to reinforce this quintet with a mass scene. Grigorovich alone devised this scene in a key consonant with the music, relying basically on Petipa's choreographic version. But this is a subject reserved for a future story.

Princess Aurora's *adagio* with four cavaliers is but the initial episode of a large-scale choreographic scene. This *adagio* is followed by the dance of the Maids of Honor and pages, which has the significance of an interlude required for relaxation and is partly of a divertissement character. At the same time, just as the waltz, it presents a characterization of Princess Aurora with her vigor, innocent cunning, and coquetry.

The next scene is Princess Aurora's extended "portrait" variation, which conveys the mood of lyrical meditation. Although this variation is very difficult for a ballerina, it is devoid of any virtuoso tricks, spectacular spins, or filigree point technique. The difficulty stems from the need for ideal precision, integrity and musicality in the performance of classical dance. Here a plastic cantilena prevails, a succession of fleeting movements alternating with soaring flights and spins. This variation culminates in *jete en tournant*.

Further, the coda conveys Princess Aurora's enjoyment of life, her fascination with her own dance, which gradually assumes a *bravura* quality. The coda completes the number and ushers in a new stage of the action: Princess Aurora catches sight of an old woman beating time with a spindle, snatches it out of her hands and, unaware of the mortal danger threatening her, plays with it merrily to the delight of the watching crowd.

No. 9. The finale. Princess Aurora accidentally injures her finger on the spindle. Her dance suddenly comes to an abrupt stop. An instant of fright is followed by a "dance of dizziness." She meanders across the stage and then sinks to the floor lifeless. All are in despair. After a brief episode of confusion Fairy Carabosse makes her appearance and quickly moves out of sight.

All this is conveyed by means of pantomime. But now one hears the Lilac Fairy's serene song that spells tranquility and hope. The fairy slowly floats over the stage. The dormant kingdom is lost to view in the growing jungle of a magic forest.

The second act presents another hero — Prince Desire, who will destroy the spell of witchcraft and awaken Princess Aurora from her eternal sleep. This act begins with a scene of hunting, the games and dances of the courtiers, who are joined by the peasants.

No. 10. An entr'acte and a scene. The trumpets play the fanfare music of the hunt. The entrée of the courtiers is followed by the entrée of Prince Desire. The entire scene is based on pantomime.

This is followed by **Number 11** — the game of hide-and-seek, **Number 12** — the dances of the Duchesses, Baronesses, Countesses and Marquises. Tchaikovsky's music here is a stylized minuet, gavotte, passe-pied, and rigadoon. **Number 13** is a peasant farandole.

The next episode is the departure of the hunting party (beginning of **Number 14**) to the music opening **Number 10**, which thus provides the leitmotif for all the episodes of this large scene.

At first glance, this succession of dances in different styles may seem a sheer divertissement. In fact, however, all these lay the musical groundwork for the events and indirectly illustrate Prince Desire's character traits, just as the dances of the Prologue and the first act were an indirect characterization of Princess Aurora. This circumstance has no choreographic expression in Petipa's production. Prince Desire is present here, it is true, but he has no dance part to play. In this scene his image is conveyed exclusively by means of pantomime.

No. 14. A scene. Its beginning (up to the figure 30 in the score) completes, in effect, the preceding large scene of the hunt. This is followed by one of the key episodes in the ballet, covering the second part of **No. 14**, as well as **Nos. 15** and **16**.

Prince Desire has a romantic dream, in which the Lilac Fairy visits him. By a motion of her magic wand she shows him the image of his promised bride fast asleep in her enchanted kingdom and then conjures up a phantom of Princess Aurora to appear before the Prince with nereids surrounding her.

Petipa choreographed the scene of Prince Desire and the Lilac Fairy as a mimic dialogue. The next episode, however, is a veritable triumph of classical and symphonic dance in *pas d'action* style.

No. 15. Pas d'action. It consists of Princess Aurora's and Prince Desire's duet, Princess Aurora's variation, and a coda. It is closely followed by **No. 16**, in which the Prince implores the Lilac Fairy to help him find and rescue the Princess.

Pas d'action is one of the pinnacles of artistry in Petipa's choreography and a specimen of symphonic *pas d'action* dance in general.

Three soloists (Prince Desire, Princess Aurora and the Lilac Fairy) and a female corps de ballet (nereids) take part in it. No words are eloquent enough to describe the beauty of the lyrical *adagio* of Princess Aurora and Prince Desire, the mastery and grace of the changing airy patterns of the corps de ballet, the consummate perfection and musicality of the entire composition.

Everything here is fluid, transient, flimsy and evasive. It is the image of a phantom called up by a miracle. In the meantime, the inner motivation of the events develops continually.

Prince Desire seeks to unite with Princess Aurora, and at one moment, she comes close to him, at another, escapes from him like an apparition.

The corps de ballet of nereids, obeying a wave of the Lilac Fairy's hand, now unites the heroes, now separates them. The fluent cantilena of the duet of Princess Aurora and Prince Desire is in sharp contrast to the hovering dance of the nereids, which is based on small leaping steps as they fill the stage with their airy ranks or fly into the wings from where they burst out in small groups again.

But now the phantom vanishes into thin air. The enchanted Prince, consumed with love, implores the Lilac Fairy to bring Princess Aurora back. Unfortunately, after the brilliant *pas d'action* in this *Number 16* Petipa again resorted to pantomime, so that the choreographic image of the Prince failed to be further developed.

It would be relevant to point out Petipa's tendency, characteristic of his art in general, to integrate a few musical numbers into a large-scale common scene. Thus, *Numbers 10-14* and *14-16* are integrated in the Second Act. The prerequisites for this are to be found in the symphonic nature of Tchaikovsky's music. On this basis Petipa enlarged choreographic episodes and created large "supernumbers" which had never existed in ballet before. This innovation would be imaginatively applied in Grigorovich's choreography.

No. 17. A panorama. Moved by the Prince's supplications, Fairy Lilac agrees to bring him to his beloved. They step into a boat which slowly carries them to the castle of the sleeping Princess. Here choreography gives way to music and spectacle: the movement of the stage scenery creates the illusion of a boat sailing over smooth waters.

However, it would be wrong to describe this episode as merely a fantastic event from a fairy tale. It is the image of charmingly beautiful nature consonant with the central theme of the ballet: the triumph of beauty and the joy of life.

The fairy and the Prince arrive at the castle which is fast asleep and overgrown with thickets. The curtains fall and the wonderful music of the entr'acte (**No. 18**) is heard, a solo violin singing of love and happiness.

No. 19. A scene of sleep. The music portrays the dormant kingdom. The theme of Fairy Carabosse sounds mysteriously and insinuatingly. In a number of productions Fairy Carabosse guards the dormant kingdom, but that was not the case in Petipa's original. The Prince gropes through the thickets towards the sleeping Princess. His kiss awakens her from her eternal slumber. The heroes come up to the proscenium to the accompaniment of jubilant music. That is the end of the second act.

It would seem the ballet could very well end with that scene. In a play just a short additional dénouement would be required. In the genre of ballet, however, the situation is different. It will be recalled that the heroes fell in love with each other, not at the instant of Aurora's awakening, but in the central dance episodes of the preceding acts. Therefore, the happy ending should be shown in elaborate musical and dance scenes. Prince Desire's kiss and Princess Aurora's awakening are simply a linking event between them.

The Third Act completes the complex and perfect construction of the ballet symphony. Its significance for the story is negligible: it is simply a festival on the occasion of the wedding of Aurora and Desire. Its message in the music and choreography, however, is of enormous importance. This is, in effect, the song of triumphant love, the assertion of beauty and the joy of life, the resolution of the conflict between good and evil forces, the victory of goodness and the apotheosis of happiness.

Thus, the Third Act is conceptually integrated with the First and Second Acts. It is the genuine outcome, conclusion and resolution of the succession of events and the central dramatic conflict.

No. 21. A march. The music is jubilant and theatrically picturesque. There are festive scenes of the entrées of the courtiers, the royal couple, and the newlyweds. The polonaise (*No. 22*), which accompanies the ceremonial entrée of the fairy tale characters, is integrated into this introductory number.

The next scene is one of the *pas de quatre* of the fairies of gold and silver and precious gems — sapphire and diamonds — consisting of an entrée, four variations and a coda. Just as in the Prologue where the fairies symbolically endowed the baby Princess with splendid character traits, now they symbolically bestow wealth on the newlyweds.

As usually happens in ballet, however, the underlying significance of this number is much wider and greater than its role in the story. The music of the quartet of the fairies of gold and silver and precious gems suggests associations with the music of the sextet of the fairies in the Prologue.

Again one hears the mellow waltz motifs and the lively scherzo-like rhythms of a polka, as well as faint echoes reminiscent of the theme of the Lilac Fairy. The music is inspired with goodness and happiness. This is the emotional realm of the newlyweds, an indirect description of their spiritual state, which is related to their union as much as the waltz in the First Act was related to Princess Aurora and the hunting scene in the First Act to Prince Desire.

As far as the choreography is concerned, every variation is a brilliant specimen of Petipa's fantasy. All of them are based on virtuoso dance and seem to sparkle with joy, although each of them retains its strikingly individual style.

The suite of the fairies of gold and silver and precious gems is followed by the so-called suite of fairytales (*Nos. 24-27*). According to Vsevolzhsky's plan, this was to be a masquerade of its own kind where every number would reproduce the subject of some of Charles Perrault's fairytales.

Tchaikovsky and Petipa, of course, created what may be called a paean of praise or a wreath of laurels for Perrault. Their conception however, was wider. Each of the numbers is a variation on the main theme of the ballet: misfortune is transient, while joy and goodness eventually triumph. Each number also reveals the different aspects of the theme of love, which is also a key motif running through the ballet. Thus, what seems at first glance a pure divertissement is not absolutely such in reality, but is a dramaturgically indispensable component required for additional elaboration of the main message of the music and the choreography.

Puss in Boots and White Pussy Cat are the first to come out on stage. Their love quarrel is a dance of feline steps and fierce scratching imitating a cat fight. They are obviously enjoying their squabble, and their duet looks like a funny love play. Illustrative elements are essential for both the music and the choreography of this scene, though they have no decisive significance. The coquetry of the lovers is the leitmotif of their dance.

The *pas de deux* of Bluebeard and Princess Florina is a dance of shared love, too. The imitative elements are conspicuous in this scene. These are roulades and twittering of song birds, broad soaring motifs in the music, winglike wavings of the arms, hovering steps and short spins in the choreography.

The key motif here is an urge to fly into the air, to soar into the freedom of the sky, which symbolizes the blossoming of mutual love destroying the charms of evil magic. This is a very popular duet which is often performed on the concert stage and included in the programmes of ballet competitions.

The duet of Cinderella and Prince Fortune in Petipa's choreography has not survived to date. In the author's conception it was to be a variation on the very same theme of love: Cinderella's pursuit by the Prince and the joy of their love union.

The children's fairy-tales of the suite are truly charming. Little Red Riding Hood hovers over the stage on points and Big Bad Wolf pursues her with angry leaps. The dance of Hop-o'-My-Thumb and his brother escaping from the ferocious man-eater is touched with childish curiosity, fear and courage at the same time.

The dance suite of the final act is opened by a duet of the heroes. (*No. 28*). This is a *pas de deux* dance consisting of *entrée*, *adagio*, two variations and a coda. The dancers are equal partners, and their duet is one of dreams which have come true and love that triumphs in the face of adversity. Their adagio is the apogee of love.

Prince Desire's variation composed in the style of a tarantella is virile and forceful, while the variation of Princess Aurora, based on the rhythm of a polka, is graceful and playful with a shade of innocent coquetry. The play of arms and hands is a conspicuous element in its choreography. The coda is a virtuoso dance in *bravura* style. The whole duet is a dance of jubilation and delight. It is also often performed at public concerts and is an indispensable item on the repertoire of all international competitions of ballet dancers.

The finale (*No. 30*), which is composed in the rhythm of a mazurka, includes a farewell ring dance of fairy-tales and a parade of all the characters. The wealth and splendor of its choreography crown the ballet.

The Sleeping Beauty is the epitome of Petipa's finest achievements in the art of choreography: a wealth of ideas and rich fantasy, broad and detailed elaboration of the language of classical dance with superlative specimens of symphonic dance based on the music. The great profundity and vividness of image characterization with strong and delicate emotions expressed in dance and great humanitarian ideals conveyed in the message of the ballet exemplify the consummate beauty and perfection of artistic form, the synthesis and integrity of the arts creating a unique ballet performance.

The Sleeping Beauty is a great milestone in the history of world choreography.

Despite such an achievement, Petipa failed to take advantage of the full range of choreographic opportunities offered by Tchaikovsky's music. This refers in the first place to his reliance on pantomime in revealing the image of Prince Desire. His dance part consists of one variation and one coda, while in other situations it is confined to the support of his female partner or to pantomime. The possibilities of symphonized dance so brilliantly brought into play in many episodes of Petipa's choreography are very much greater in the music. Nevertheless, *The Sleeping Beauty* is one of the summits of world ballet.

Yuri Grigorovich made this comment on the significance of Petipa's artistic legacy.

"Participation in a Petipa ballet means the joy of genuine creativity and enormous professional advancement to any performer. Petipa was endowed with a truly unique understanding of the dancer's artistic aptitudes, and in his choreography he presented them in the most favorable light, not at the expense of the ballet but to its best advantage.

"There are many examples to illustrate my point, and in *The Sleeping Beauty* they are especially numerous. Such a masterpiece as the scenes of the fairies of gold and silver and precious gems in which organic integrity, the logic of movement, and the sense of the architectonics of classical dance are brought to the superior degree of perfection is a striking specimen of his genius.

"There are choreographers who are more proficient in various forms of solo dance. Some ballet masters have a propensity to composing ensemble dances. The uniqueness of Petipa's talent stemmed from his superlative mastery of all forms of

44

dance regardless of whether it was intended for the première, a soloist or the corps de ballet.

"Such compositions as the fairies in the Prologue to *The Sleeping Beauty*, the Shadows in *La Bayadére*, the nereids in *The Sleeping Beauty* are unexcelled specimens of symphonic choreography to this day."

It is hard to add anything to these words. Indeed, they belong to an artist who feels the greatest reverence for Petipa and has deepened and developed his traditions.

Gallery of Interpreters

PRINCESS AURORA

Lyubov Roslavleva.
1899.

Yekaterina Geltzer.
1899.

Nina Podgoretskaya.
1924.

Marina Semyonova.
1930.

Sofia Golovkina.
1937.

Raisa Struchkova.
1952.

Maya Plisetskaya.
1952.

Irina Tikhomirnova.
1952.

Marina Kondratyeva.
1963.

Nina Timofeyeva. 1964.

Yekaterina Maximova.
1973.

Nina Sorokina. 1974
(Vladimir Tikhonov as Prince).

A Look At Stage History

Immediately after its première *The Sleeping Beauty* became a favorite item in the repertoire and was invariably a success. In Moscow, however, it was staged as late as January 1899 by the choreographer A.A. Gorsky who had transferred Petipa's production to the Bolshoi.

The playbills of its Moscow première announced: "This ballet is presented on the Moscow stage by Mr. Gorsky, an artist of the St. Petersburg Imperial Theaters, by the ballet notation system of V.I. Stepanov." This system had evidently proved very helpful to Gorsky, although he was thoroughly familiar with the production. In fact he had start his Russian career in St. Petersburg and taken part in Petipa's ballets.

Gorsky faithfully reproduced Petipa's choreography. To save funds, however, the final apotheosis was deleted from the production. The principal innovation was the new stage scenery painted by A.F. Geltzer and K.F. Waltz, well-known artists of the Bolshoi and past masters of fantastic décor.

The panorama painted by Geltzer was unusually picturesque and admired by everybody. When preparing it, the artist had drawn numerous sketches and invented scenes relying on his imagination. He embodied all this material in a stage setting of magic poetry.

At the Moscow Bolshoi *The Sleeping Beauty* was as successful as it had been in St. Petersburg, and it was performed twenty-four times during its first year run.

The part of Princess Aurora was danced by the well-known ballerina L.A. Roslavleva. Her technique was comparable in brilliance to that of Brianza, who had performed this part in St. Petersburg, but Roslavleva enriched it with her profoundly Russian interpretation of the music.

Critics wrote about her as follows: "Roslavleva was a classical dancer in the literal sense. She was endowed with a gift for linking up the old school with the modern one, that is, she embraced the modern requirements of the art of ballet without breaking with the time-honored traditions in dance. Whatever she did on stage was beautiful. That harmony of movements, impeccable lines, intent gaze, and innocent smile led one to think of the beauty and integrity of her inner self. Roslavleva was justly called a brilliant star of Russian and world ballet."

On the Moscow stage *The Sleeping Beauty* in this version survived until 1936. In St. Petersburg the ballet was renewed after a brief interval by A.A. Gorsky in 1914. Only a few minor details were revised in the choreography. The decor and costumes, however, were the work of K.A. Korovin. Though he was one of the finest artists of his time both in the genre of theatrical decoration and in easel painting, his stage scenery for *The Sleeping Beauty* was not among his best achievements as eyewitnesses reported that the decor was much too ordinary.

Stylization in the manner of 17th-century French art had disappeared and the charm of a poetical fairytale was also gone. A critic wrote: "In the renewal of 1914 *The Sleeping Beauty* lost much of its charm. The extremely bad décor and costumes left nothing of the enchanting fairytale so poetically worked out in the minutest detail in the original production. The flame in the fireplace, the grotto with a cascade from which the Lilac Fairy emerged, the lovely panorama painted by Bocharov were all gone, and the dusty spiderweb in Princess Aurora's bedroom was replaced with an absurd tangle of ivy, which could have grown anywhere but inside a palace."

That version of *The Sleeping Beauty* remained in the repertoire during the first five years after the revolution. Although no substantial revisions were made in its choreography, the message of the ballet, its profound idea content and dramaturgical conception were steadily relegated to the background, while its character as a *divertissement* came to the forefront.

In 1922 there was another renewal of *The Sleeping Beauty* undertaken by F.V. Lopukhov, a leading Soviet choreographer. First of all, he took steps to free Petipa's original choreography from all later adulterations. For instance, Aurora's gentle lyrical variation in the *pas d'action* of the Second Act (No. 15 b) had been at one time replaced at Marina Kseszinska's request with a different one, in bravura style.

Lopukhov restored Tchaikovsky's original music and Petipa's choreography. In the First Act he revived the crowd taking part in the scene of Aurora's playing with the spindle. He also restored some deletions made in Tchaikovsky's score in the 1914 production by lengthening, in particular, the scene of the knitting maidens at the beginning of the First Act.

Lopukhov composed anew the Lilac Fairy's variation in the Prologue which had been forgotten by that time, presented a new choreography of the dances in the scene of the hunt in the Second Act, and the entrée of the fairies in the Third Act where the main heroes appear in the dance along with the fairies.

Lopukhov also restored the musical entr'acts before the scene of Aurora's awakening and staged the scene of Fairy Carabosse with her rats to the music of the "dormant kingdom".

PRINCESS FLORINE

49

Yelizaveta Anderson.
1890.

Vera Mosolova.
1906.

Zinaida Vasilyeva.
1936.

Svetlana Adyrkhayeva.
1964.

PRINCE CHARMING

Irina Prokofyeva.
1974.

Vasily Tikhomirov. 1899.

Alexander Volinin.
1908.

Lavrenty Novikov.
1912.

Viktor Smoltsov.
1925.

Leonid Zhukov.
1927.

Vladimir Preobrazhensky.
1944.

Yuri Kondratov.
1952.

49

Boris Khokhlov. 1954.

Vladimir Tikhonov. 1964.

Maris Liepa. 1973.

Galina Petrova. 1936.

Lyudmila Cherkasova. 1952.

Rimma Karelskaya. 1952.

Mariana Bogolyubskaya. 1973.

Marina Leonova. 1973.

THE CARABOSSE FAIRY

Tatyana Golikova. 1973.

Viktorina Kriger. 1937.

Yelena Vanke. 1952.

Vladimir Levashov. 1973.

50

For all the positive significance of this work *The Sleeping Beauty* was not reborn in that production, because the integral artistic conception of the ballet was not given a fresh or more profound interpretation.

In the 1920s and 1930s, the outstanding Soviet ballerinas M.T. Semenova, G.S. Ulanova, N.M. Dudinskaya, O.G. Iordan, T.M. Vecheslova, F.I. Balabina and others breathed new life into the part of Princess Aurora. They lent her image lifelike human features, cheerfulness and inspiration. That was an indisputable achievement of the Soviet ballet theater. The ballet as a whole, however, increasingly assumed the features of a museum piece, while the part of Prince Desire continued to rely on pantomime, and the profound symphonic idea of Tchaikovsky's music was not fully revealed.

The Moscow productions of 1936 by the choreographers A.M. Messerer and A.I. Chekrygin with I.M. Rabinovich as the stage designer failed to introduce anything fundamentally new into the ballet. That was equally true of the production of 1952 staged by the choreographers M.M. Gabovich and A.M. Messerer with M.A. Obolensky and L.N. Silich as stage designers. Both productions were based on Petipa's choreography, though occasional attempts were made to supplement it, for instance, to reinforce Aurora's adagio with four cavaliers by adding a few dancing pairs in the background and to illustrate the scene of Carabosse's prophecy with children's figures depicting the predicted events. There was also some effort to lend more emphasis to dance in the part of Prince Desire.

In the 1954 production a special curtain with a painted scene of the contest between the Lilac Fairy and Fairy Carabosse was used in the Prologue. In the action, however, the meaning of their conflict was not adequately revealed. The choreographers had paid too much attention to the lifelike representation of events to the detriment of the fantastic in the fairy-tale in an effort to make the story more realistic.

The production of *The Sleeping Beauty* by K.M. Sergeyev at the Kirov Theater of Leningrad in 1952 was more significant. The choreography continued his quest for ways to give more dancing to the part of Prince Desire, in the scene of the hunt, in particular.

This production threw into salient relief the brilliant talent of N.M. Dudinskaya, I.A. Kolpakova, A.I. Sizova, and G.G. Komleva who danced the part of Aurora at different times.

The artist S.B. Virsaladze painted for the ballet wonderful stage scenery with a hall in baroque style in the Prologue, a luxuriant park in the First Act, the flaming golden autumn in the scene of the hunt, a magnificent panorama and a shining palace in the final act. It would be no exaggeration to say that in the stage history of this ballet this scenery was more beautiful, poetical and consonant with Tchaikovsky's music that of any earlier production.

K.M. Sergeyev sought to preserve Petipa's choreography as faithfully as possible. At first, he added some new details to it. For instance, in Fairy Violent's variation he replaced the position where she sharply throws her arm forward with an extended index finger by a more graceful gesture, introduced some upper supports in the *pas d'action* of the Second Act, and other details. Later, however, he deleted all of them, having realized the consummate perfection of Petipa's choreographic discoveries.

This production is still alive on the Leningrad stage and was released in a screen version in 1964.

The Sleeping Beauty has been staged in many countries of the world. All these productions are based on Petipa's choreography. Too often, however, they are arbitrarily modernized with the result that the style, imagery and message of the ballet are distorted.

A genuine ballet lover would hardly be pleased to see Prince Desire in blue jeans.

In 1922, S.P. Diaghilev produced a one-act version entitled *"The Wedding of the Sleeping Beauty,"* and in 1948 S. Lifar staged the Third Act under the name of *Divertissement* at the Grand Opera in Paris. One-act versions were produced in other countries as well. Though they have Petipa's brilliant dances preserved, they dilute the essence of the ballet.

The original *Sleeping Beauty* was never intended for a divertissement or a concert. Tchaikovsky and Petipa sought to make dance dramaturgically meaningful, and the ballet as a whole conceptually profound and consistent with their humanitarian ideals.

Grigorovich's Role in Ballet

Yuri Nikolayevich Grigorovich (b. 1927) is one of the world's leading contemporary choreographers. During his record of thirty-odd years in the field he has created eleven large ballet productions, numerous works and dances in operas, and has been chief choreographer of the Bolshoi since 1964.

When Grigorovich decided to produce his own version of *The Sleeping Beauty*, he was already a mature choreographer adhering to a definite set of artistic principles. Before analyzing his production, therefore, a story of his art and a definition of its essence would be relevant here.

A spectator who has seen one of Grigorovich's ballets will certainly note its profound idea content and philosophical message, an artistic interpretation of important moral and psychological problems, its life-like and vivid human characters, as well as a variety of choreographic forms, a wealth of imaginative dance styles, sophisticated choreographic patterns, a rich dance language, and a colorful palette of means of expression.

Therefore, any of his ballets produces a strong artistic impression on the audience and conveys a great humanitarian and moral ideal. Suffice it to recall the vivid and original artistic interpretation of the theme of the artist and reality in *The Stone Flower* and the wide variety and complexity of moral and psychological collisions expressed in the artist's love of the people as the supreme manifestation of humaneness.

The Legend of Love presents the images of violence and oppression and the struggle for freedom.

Spartacus is a heroic tragedy with a message of freedom addressed to all humanity. *Ivan the Terrible* is dedicated to the idea of struggle for Russian statehood against the background of historical events and moral ordeals. *The Angara* and *The Golden Age* handle the moral and psychological problems facing young people today. Classical ballets have also received a more profound interpretation in Grigorovich's art.

For their profound idea content Grigorovich's ballets are superior to whatever was achieved in this genre before him. This has been made possible by his strenuous efforts to develop the language and forms of choreographic art itself.

Foreign ballet lovers and choreographers admiring the philosophical profundity and wealth of dance fantasy and forms in his productions are not always clearly aware of Grigorovich's innovative ideas and reforms in the very structure of a ballet production, which have had a strong impact on all contemporary choreography. To fully appreciate this innovation one should know the following two circumstances in the history of Soviet ballet.

In the period between 1930 and 1950 Soviet choreographers were fascinated with the idea of bringing ballet closer to drama and attached singular significance to the mastery of art direction and acting in a ballet production. This gave rise to the genre of dramatic ballet, in which an extended dramatic plot and true-to-life relations between human characters were regarded as important, while symphonic dance with its complex polyphonic and ensemble forms was absent or nearly absent; pantomime prevailed in the performance, while dance was steadily losing ground.

Some ballets in this genre were quite successful. Among them were *The Fountain of Bakhchisarai* by Boris Asafiev in Rostislav Zakharov's choreography (1934) and *Romeo and Juliet* by Sergei Prokofiev in Leonid Lavrovsky's choreography (1940). However, the steady deterioration of dance forms and the prevalence of pantomime soon caused general dissatisfaction, and even the symptoms of a crisis in ballet which became strikingly manifest in the 1950s.

On the other hand, the genre of symphonic ballet, that is, a choreographic production based on symphonic music not intended for dance and interpreted with or without reference to a particular subject, had taken shape in Russia as far back as pre-revolutionary times. Its founding fathers were Michel Fokine, Alexander Gorsky and L. Myasin.

In the 1920s ballets of this kind were staged by Fedor Lopukhov (*The Greatness of the Universe* to the music of Ludwig van Beethoven's Fourth Symphony, 1923). Later the symphonic ballet was forgotten, although in the West it was preserved and developed by George Balanchine and many other choreographers. In the early 1960s symphonic ballet was revived in the Soviet Union (*Leningrad Symphony* to the music of Dmitri Shostakovich's *Seventh Symphony* in I. Belsky's choreography, 1961, and others).

Before Grigorovich, dramatic and symphonic ballets had existed separately and independently from each other, just as they often exist today. Grigorovich was the first to integrate and synthesize them into a common whole.

His productions of *The Stone Flower* by Sergei Prokofiev (1957), *The Legend of Love* by S. Melikov (1959), *Spartacus* by Aram Khachaturian (1968), *Ivan the Terrible* by Sergei Prokofiev (1974), and other ballets preserve the basic plot, a thoroughly planned dramaturgy, lifelike human characters, and true-to-life relations between the heroes. This realistic and philosophic content, however, is revealed by bringing ballet closer not so much to drama as to music.

His ballets are based on large choreographic scenes, each of which is a stage, a turning-point or the culmination in the development not so much of the external action as the inner drama.

These scenes in themselves present an uninterrupted, continuous development of dance, just as in symphonic ballet, on the principles analogous to those of music, that is, by creating a polyphonic structure, by developing a theme, by sustaining undulating increases and decreases in dance and by securing an integral common culmination. The choreography does not illustrate the music or the drama but absorbs them, as it were, and becomes the focus of their synthesis.

Yuri Grigorovich inside the Bolshoi Hall in Moscow.

The synthesis of dramatic and symphonic ballet opened new artistic opportunities for combining philosophic profundity and image content with generous creativity in dance, a wealth of choreographic forms and styles, and the supreme achievements in symphonized dance. It may be argued that this synthesis best agrees with the nature and specific features of the art of ballet and hence is a matter of course. This is certainly true. However, it is very hard to achieve in practical choreography, much harder than to stage, say, a pure dramatic ballet or a dance symphony, so it was Grigorovich's genuine artistic discovery.

Dramatic and symphonic ballets staged by the world's best choreographers exist, as a rule, independently from one another. Take, for instance, *Romeo and Juliet* and *The Classical Symphony* of Leonid Lavrovsky, The *Prodigal Son* and *The Crystal Palace* of George Balanchine, *The Taming of the Shrew* and *Brahms' Concerto* of G. Cranko, *The Child and Magic* and *Janacek's Symphonietta* of I. Kilian, *Don Giovanni* and *Mozart's Symphony* of D. Neuemaier. This is, of course, quite reasonable. The synthesis of these principles, which has been achieved by Grigorovich for the first time in 20th-century choreography affords ballet new, rich, artistic opportunities.

This synthesis was already appreciable in Petipa's romantic ballet. Grigorovich revived and developed these traditions on a new foundation. He found Petipa's ideas very similar to his own. Whereas before Grigorovich, Petipa's traditions had been often underestimated or even discarded by choreographers, now their significance for modern ballet has come to light. Grigorovich has developed these traditions and advanced them to a higher level, combining them with his bold innovative ideas.

"What is the most significant factor in the art of a great master?" he asks rhetorically, "What is consonant with our aspirations, hopes and conceptions? This is primarily symphonization of dance. When young choreographers of today are trying to establish the polyphonic principles in choreography, one should not think they are starting from scratch.

"They rely on Petipa's experience, on the principles he formulated, and on the traditions sanctified by his name. When any of the figures prominent in the art of ballet is trying to solve the problem of musical and choreographic dramaturgy, his experiment is based, with rare exceptions, on the art of Petipa who has left us specimens of a masterly solution to such problems.

"These are not samples for blind imitation but for an independent quest and for free reflection consistent with the lessons of the classical heritage."

Grigorovich has followed these principles in his choreography of his own new productions and in producing a revival of *The Sleeping Beauty*.

Grigorovich's First Version of The Sleeping Beauty

Grigorovich's first production of *The Sleeping Beauty* dates back to the year 1963. By that time he had already choreographed two ballets which were a great success with the public but aroused fierce controversy among ballet critics. These were *The Stone Flower* by Sergei Prokofiev and *The Legend of Love* by A. Melikov.

The Sleeping Beauty was the first classical ballet he was invited to stage at the Bolshoi. Before that he had worked at the Kirov Theater of Leningrad.

To understand the conception of that first experiment a few words about the situation in the field of Soviet ballet which prevailed at the time would be relevant. It was a time of heated debates between champions of dramatized ballet, known as "choreodrama" in the jargon of Soviet ballet critics which reigned supreme in Soviet choreography between 1930 and 1950, and champions of a new trend in ballet, who advocated symphonized dance to be brought closer to the music and a revival of Petipa's traditions. They opposed genre scenes on the ballet stage, naturalism, the domination of pantomime, and underestimation of the historically developed variety of choreographic language and forms.

This new trend was spearheaded by Grigorovich and had a large following among choreographers and critics.

Grigorovich conceived *The Sleeping Beauty* as a polemic ballet to a certain extent. His idea was to display the wealth of dance forms devised by Petipa and to present them as a spectacular concert of its own kind. He intended to prove that a ballet performance can exist on the basis of symphonic dance alone. Therefore, he expunged pantomime and genre scenes, made the images of Prince Desire and Fairy Carabosse dancing parts, and choreographed the latter's role in purely classical style.

Despite his profound respect for Petipa, Grigorovich proceeded from his own set of principles regarding the classical heritage which he would later describe in one of his articles:

"Times are changing, aesthetic criteria are in a state of flux, and we ourselves are changing, too. The rule of the times is a cruel rule. Ballets are growing older and obsolescent.... But what is becoming obsolescent in the first place?

It is the conventional non-rhythmic pantomime obstructing the action and interfering with the clear-cut pattern of the general composition of the production.

The fragments of symphonic choreography are the basis for the dramaturgy of the ballet to which all other plastic forms are subordinated.

Is it possible to remake Petipa's ballets? The choreographer himself gave the answer to this question. He proved more conclusively than anybody else that old productions have to be revised sooner or later. The result of careful reconstruction varies with the talent of the choreographer who has undertaken this effort."

The principles put forward by Grigorovich were progressive principles which were bound to advance the art of ballet. In the heat of a polemic over their practical implementation, however, Grigorovich carried something too far.

For instance, since he had discarded pantomime and character genre dances, he deleted the beginning of The First Act (scene of knitting maidens), the beginning of The Second Act (scene of picnic and hunt) and the beginning of The Third Act (march, polonaise, entrées of courtiers and fairy-tale characters).

In our day, it is, of course, necessary and possible to renounce the naive methods of conventional pantomime in old ballets (explanation by gestures and symbolic signs). It is necessary and possible to fight against the predominance of pantomime in a ballet production, just as to oppose the trend towards vulgar genre interpretation of the action. All this has really become old-fashioned. It would definitely be wrong, however, to renounce pantomime and character genre dance in general, and, in particular, *The Sleeping Beauty*.

Indeed, this will cause a serious disturbance in its dramaturgy. If real-life genre scenes are deleted from a production, the opposition of poetry to prose, of dreams to reality, of the ideal to real life will vanish, the interrelationship between the fantastic and real life typical of romantic ballet will be obscured.

It is not so much the question of outward contrasts disappearing from the production, which thus becomes somewhat monotonous, as one of losing the tension of the inner conflict with the result that symphonic choreography itself begins to gravitate towards a suite.

Grigorovich's desire to lend emphasis to dance in the parts of Prince Desire and Fairy Carabosse was reasonable. In his second production of *The Sleeping Beauty* he choreographed them with superior brilliance. He had introduced some innovations in his first production, it is true, but he had also committed some errors.

It was hardly reasonable, for instance, to hand over the variation of the Maids of Honor and pages in the First Act to the four cavaliers. As far as the part of Fairy Carabosse is concerned, its choreography on the basis of pure classical dance softened the contrast between her and the Lilac Fairy and hence detracted from the impression produced by the principal conflict.

In his effort to prove that dance could provide the final solution to all problems, Grigorovich attempted to present the scenes of the overgrowth covering the castle with a jungle forest and the panorama in the language of dance. In other words, he added choreographic effects to the stage spectacle. That was indisputably an original and interesting innovation. Nevertheless, it failed to impress the audience and left the choreographer himself disappointed.

In the scene of the overgrowth covering the castle a few fairies crossed the stage by long *jeté* steps, while in the panorama for *pas de bourée* flocks of maidens floated past in neat files as though symbolizing a farewell to the heroes.

This production of *The Sleeping Beauty* was a bold experimental ballet based on novel artistic principles. However, it was not yet perfect, at certain places was carried to extremes, and partly contradicted the musical and choreographic dramaturgy of Tchaikovsky and Petipa.

Therefore, Grigorovich himself was not completely satisfied with it, so in exactly ten years, in 1973, he returned to this ballet and produced at the Bolshoi a truly brilliant masterpiece, the finest in the stage history of this ballet, which has won broad popularity with ballet-going audiences in the Soviet Union and the rest of the world.

Yuri Grigorovich outside the Bolshoi Hall in Moscow.

Music, Dance and Dramaturgy

To be able to make a fair assessment of Grigorovich's final production of *The Sleeping Beauty*, it is necessary to take another look at the musical and choreographic dramaturgy of Tchaikovsky and Petipa. We have already discussed it in considerable detail, analyzing the composer's music and the choreography of its first producer.

Now we need not only to sum up the discussion but also to emphasize both the ideological profundity and image content of this dramaturgy, as well as its impeccable proportions and logical perfection, because its complete expression became the starting point and basis of Grigorovich's splendid production.

The identical structural type of all acts of *The Sleeping Beauty* is another quality that merits attention. Every act is focused on its own central event and has its own emotional key. All of them are quite distinct; what is more, they are so contrastive that the spectator never has the impression of monotony. At the same time, the principle of their construction is uniform and is based on a synthesis of the music and the dramaturgy.

Every act has its own culmination. The opening scenes which introduce the characters (entrées of the courtiers, the fairies, the festival guests, etc.) are followed by divertissement dances, which transform into a large classical ensemble leading up to the active finale.

The logic of the ballet dramaturgy can be illustrated by the following scheme:

INTRODUCTION

Prologue:	Introduction	Divertissement (courtiers, fairies)	Ensemble (pas de six)	Finale
First Act:	Introduction	Divertissement (grand waltz)	Ensemble (grand pas)	Finale
Second Act:	Introduction	Divertisement (dances at picnic)	Ensemble (pas d'action)	Finale
Third Act:	Introduction	Divertissement (precious gems, fairytales)	Ensemble (pas de deux)	Finale

The introduction and the apotheosis provide a frame for the ballet. Both these episodes are outside the action. The music of the introduction conveys the main conflict (collision between the themes of good and evil — between the Lilac Fairy and Fairy Carabosse), anticipating its embodiment on the stage. The apotheosis means the resolution of this conflict and the triumph of goodness.

The development of the action brings to light a definite structural law which has a profound dramaturgical meaning. Let us examine it in greater detail.

None of the acts begins from a definite state, and whatever takes place during further development happens before the eyes of the audience. This makes it possible to provide an acceleration to the main events and to trace the common dynamic line more distinctly.

The initial scene of every act presents the entrée and assembly of the main characters taking part in the action. In the Prologue this is the entrée of the royal couple; the courtiers and the guests assembled to celebrate Princess Aurora's birth (march, No. 1).

The First Act presents the entrée of the knitting maidens, Cattalabutte and the King and the next scene with the knitting maidens (scene, No. 5).

The Second Act presents the entrée of the hunting party, the ladies and Prince Desire who are gathering together for a picnic (scene, No. 10).

The Third Act presents the entrée of the festival guests and the fairytale characters (march and polonaise, Nos. 21 and 22). The music of all these introductory scenes has a festive, marchlike character (in the Second Act the marchlike theme follows the theme of the hunt). It implies presenting on the stage the scene of a procession in which the decisive role is played not so much by the plastic means of dance as of pantomime. The dance reveals the predominance of character and folk genre elements.

The introductory scenes in every act are followed by dance episodes and scenes of a divertissement character. In the Prologue this is the "scene with dances" (No. 2) consisting of three episodes: the dance entrée of the fairies (F-dur, music reminiscent of a lullaby), the entrée of the Lilac Fairy (A-dur, music of an impassioned lyrical character), and an episode which is marked in the libretto as a "dance of maidens and pages" (A-dur, graceful miniature waltz).

In the First Act the scene with the knitting maidens transforms into the famous grand waltz B-dur (No. 6), which expresses the common joy preceding the entrée of Princess Aurora. In the Second Act the entrée of the courtiers and the Prince is followed by the large suite of games and dances at the picnic. In the Third Act, the scene of general assembly is completed by two divertissements of precious gems (No. 23) and fairy-tales (Nos. 24-27) following each other.

In all these episodes the action acquires greater stability and shape than in the initial scene. It is not created in the process but runs its course. However, the background of the main events is mostly portrayed here, the milieu of the action characterized, and its general atmosphere conveyed.

This atmosphere is always festive, but its character is different in every act. These differences depend on the subsequent events and these scenes seem to herald them. The main characters have not yet come on the scene but their forthcoming appearance is anticipated in the music.

Therefore, in the Prologue it is gently lyrical (before the scene of the fairies bestowing their gifts on Aurora), in the First Act it is cheerful and playful (before the scene of Aurora and the Prince), and in the Third Act it is a jubilant fanfare (before the duet of triumphant love).

The musical and dramaturgical character of the initial scene suggested a combination of dance and pantomime. The scenes of the divertissement are fully based on dance. The music, however, suggests here to a still greater extent the prevalence of character dance (folk genre dance) and grotesque character dance over pure classical dance, although the latter is also introduced where the good fairies take part in the events.

Divertissement scenes further transform into large dance ensembles which are the culmination of the musical dramaturgy of every act. Here the images of the main heroes are revealed, and their relations develop.

In the Prologue the scene of the fairies bringing their gifts to Aurora's cradle (pas de six, No. 3) presents, in effect, an indirect characterization of the future heroine, because every fairy seems to bestow upon the baby girl her own human traits of character, such as gentleness, simple-heartedness, cheerfulness, vigor, etc. This scene begins with a gently lyrical adagio of all the fairies, includes the variation of each of them (little lyrical miniatures, a kind of "portraits" in dance), in particular, the broad and smooth variation of the Lilac Fairy and culminates in a merry dance.

In the First Act the "portrait" of young Aurora is revealed in a large scene reminiscent in shape of a *grand pas* (No. 8). It consists of Aurora's adagio with four cavaliers, suitors for her hand, the "insert" variation of the Maids of Honor and pages, Princess Aurora's variation, and a coda. Especially remarkable here is the *adagio* whose jubilant and solemn music, based on powerful life-asserting motifs, sounds like a triumphant hymn.

In the Second Act, Princess Aurora appears among the nereids as a phantom. Fairy Lilac conjures up her image to awaken love emotions in the heart of Prince Desire who is destined to break the spell of the evil Fairy Carabosse and arouse Aurora from her eternal sleep. This is a large scene (*pas d'action*), in which the duet of

Princess Aurora and Prince Desire develops with the participation of the corps de ballet (nereids) and the Lilac Fairy. The broad, lucid melody of the cellos portrays the love of Aurora and the Prince, while Aurora's playful and graceful variation adds a new trait to her image.

In the Third Act Aurora and Prince Desire dance an extended duet (*pas de deux*), which has been described as the song of triumphant love. It includes the majestic and picturesque *adagio*, the impassioned variation of the Prince, the playful and graceful variation of Princess Aurora, and a jubilant coda. This virtuoso duet in bravura style glorifies the dedication and self-sacrifice of the heroes, the triumph of love, goodness and happiness.

Since all these scenes concentrate in themselves the inner motivations of events and show the birth and development of the main heroes' love, classical dance reigns supreme here, expressing their inner world.

This dance assumes sophisticated forms conveying its sophisticated content. Dance ensembles are based on the symphonic principle, that is, they follow the guidelines set by the musical form. The polyphonic combination of the dance lines of the soloists, the coryphées and the corps de ballet, the expression, imitation and development of the dance motifs, the alternation of tension and relaxation — all this creates a complex choreographic fabric highly sensitive to the twists and turns of the lyrical drama.

The crucial significance of these scenes in every act is expressed in particular in their links with the preceding and subsequent events. These dance ensembles are united with the preceding divertissement scenes in two-part cycles of their own kind, which may be likened to the "prelude-fugue" musical cycle.

This likeness has a few foundations. For their emotional tone the divertissement episodes are largely preliminary to ensemble episodes, which express a similar state presented, however, with greater concentration and forcefulness. At the same time, the dance fabric of the divertissements is more "homophonic," so to say, and that of the ensembles is polyphonic, which is typical precisely of the "prelude-fugue" relationship.

In every act the two-part cycle (divertissement-ensemble) occupies the central position and is framed with the introduction and the finale. The ensembles are in the third quarter of the act in accordance with their culmination role and special significance for revealing the inner motivations of the action.

Let us recall the significance of the "third quarter" in the musical form. This is the most "active" episode of musical development, which usually contains some important "event" (structural fragmentation, theme elaboration, culmination, modulation, tonal shift, etc.).

In *The Sleeping Beauty* the third quarter of every act is the "lyrical focus" of the action and the culmination of developments in the inner world. Thus, the structure of the action is made consonant with the laws of the musical form. This is one of the manifestations of the synthesis of music and dramaturgy.

The external action of the ballet is best expressed in the finales. The culmination of the inner action (ensembles) seems to lead to a "breakthrough" of the action towards the finales, where the events of the story are developed with the greatest intensity.

In the Prologue and the First Act the finales are based on a direct conflict between Fairy Carabosse and the Lilac Fairy. They seem to repeat visibly the bitter conflict portrayed in the introduction musically. Thus, a line of communication between the music and the plot is established between the introduction and these finales.

The finale of the Second Act also presents a conflict between Fairy Carabosse and the Lilac Fairy, the latter emerging victorious. Therefore, the finale of the Second Act is the most extended one. It comprises a complete story (Nos. 16-20), which tranforms into an almost independent scene.

The Prince implores the Lilac Fairy to take him to Princess Aurora, and the fairy leads him into the sleeping kingdom (panorama). There is a scene of the kingdom preceded by a symphonic entr'acte. This scene is followed by the scene in which the Prince awakens Aurora with a kiss, and a jubilant conclusion.

Despite an abundance of episodes this finale is based on the integrity of the symphonic development of the music. The action of the finales is disturbed only in the Third Act where the story ends. This is the only finale devoid of an inner conflict. It is a merry common dance growing into an apotheosis.

As we see, in every act of *The Sleeping Beauty* a strict and clear cut succession of structural elements combines with a continuous thorough development. This structure has features of an integral musical form (introduction, "prelude-fugue" cycle, culmination in the third quarter, coda). Such development is distinguished by symphonic features (uniform line of emotional uplift and dynamic escalation).

The scheme presented at the beginning of our analysis can now be supplemented:

General structure:	Introduction	Divertissement	Ensemble	Finale
Dramaturgy:	Preparation for action	Background for action	Inner action	External action
Music:	March-procession	Genre dances	Symphonic dances, adagio	Through development
Choreography:	Predominance of pantomime	Predominance of character dance	Classical dance	Action scene

A Model Production

But how was this remarkable work interpretated in Yuri Grigorovich's new production? Indeed, the consonance of the choreography and the entire stage action with the musical dramaturgy is the basic criterion for assessing the ballet. The basis for this unity was laid by Petipa jointly with Tchaikovsky, who composed the music in accordance with the choreographer's conception. In Grigorovich's production this unity is reinforced by inspiring and enriching the ballet with a modern interpretation and modern methods of art direction.

In this production Petipa's precious heritage is thoroughly preserved and presented in its full wealth and brilliance. Grigorovich has taken advantage of whatever is valuable in this heritage and restored many episodes and details of the original choreography omitted in the preceding production.

At the same time, this is neither a simple specimen of restoration work, nor mechanical copy nor a museum piece. Petipa's heritage has been supplemented and developed, given a more profound interpretation, and modern methods of choreography have been employed in staging the ballet.

Composing the missing episodes of the original production and developing much of what was planned by Petipa, Grigorovich has done it with such faultless tact and a keen sense of style that it is impossible to discern the boundary between the art of the composer and the art of the choreographer unless one knows the choreographic text exactly.

The reason for that is Grigorovich's strong attraction to Petipa's choreography, which is one of the main sources of his own art. Therefore, Grigorovich has not simply restored the original production of *The Sleeping Beauty* but has produced it anew as his own version. Petipa's choreography forms an organic part of Grigorovich's production.

This is one of the paradoxes of artistic creativity. In his earlier production Grigorovich went out of his way to obliterate his individuality and reproduce Petipa's finest achievements almost literally but in fact he distorted his conception. In his new production, however, Grigorovich displayed greater creativity, regarding it as his own version, yet developing and deepening Petipa's choreography.

Evidently, in the art of ballet, individual interpretation may be likened to a rendition of music: the more faithful a pianist's interpretation of the composer's text, the greater his possibilities for self-expression, whereas an arbitrary attitude to the music is likely to lead to its false interpretation.

In his new production Grigorovich has almost completely restored Petipa's original choreography but at the same time he has created a new ballet based on a modern conception.

How did it prove possible? This writer will try to explain it. The spectator perceives a ballet performance as a well-proportioned and perfectly integral whole. Therefore, he is not concerned about the respective contributions of Grigorovich and Petipa. But the reader may find it interesting to learn more about them.

In Grigorovich's production Petipa's original choreography has been preserved in the part of Princess Aurora, all large classical ensembles (only a few new details have been added here), the waltz, the divertissement of precious gems and the fairy-tale characters (except Cinderella).

Grigorovich has created the introductory scenes and the finales of all acts, the first half of the Second Act (up to the entrée of Aurora), as well as the dance of Cinderella and Prince Fortune from the fairy tales of the Third Act, which has not survived to date.

The most fundamental innovations, however, are linked with what has been developed on the basis outlined by Petipa rather than what has been choreographed anew. This refers in the first place to the images of Fairy Carabosse and Prince Desire. In the new production they have been made more meaningful by deepening the philosophical message of the ballet, intensifying the conflict between good and evil, and reinforcing the psychological aspect of the image content. This in turn has brought the ballet closer to Tchaikovsky's music and made it possible to express it in dance with superior artistry and persuasion never witnessed before.

In Petipa's production the image of Fairy Carabosse was presented by means of pantomime by a male dancer. This was meant to emphasize the striking contrast between this image and that of Fairy Lilac: pantomime versus classical dance, the grotesque dance of an ugly witch versus perfection and harmony, the onslaught of evil powers versus the charm of gentleness and cordiality.

However, pantomime alone in a ballet so rich in dance was insufficient and tended to regulate this image to the background. Therefore, choreographers had long searched for its resolution in dance.

In his first production Grigorovich had attempted to express the contrast between the good and evil fairies, relying exclusively on classical dance. As a result this contrast was blurred, and the images of Fairy Carabosse and Fairy Lilac became so similar that at times they could be differentiated not so much by dance as by costume.

In his new production the choreographer eliminated this flaw. However, he did not simply restore Petipa's original choreography but enriched it with the experience of his earlier dance solution.

The part of Fairy Carabosse was returned to a male dancer, but now it was not based exclusively on pantomime but enriched with dance. This part is now more rhythmic and "set to music," the movements of Fairy Carabosse are more regular, varied and dancing. To use musical terms, it may now be said that in Petipa's version it was a *secco* recitative, while in Grigorovich's version it is an accompanied recitative close to an *arioso*.

Incidentally, a choreographic accompaniment exists here not only in a figurative but also in a literal sense. Fairy Carabosse has her own retinue of three ugly dwarfs and three rats dressed in old women's clothes and holding reticules in their claws (very much like the charity dwellers in *The Queen of Spades* but in this scene generalized to the degree of a symbol).

In the grotesque dances of Fairy Carabosse her retinue perform the role of a corps de ballet. Now they keep close to their wicked mistress, now they spring away from her or follow her like a trail. In the Prologue where Fairy Carabosse, seized with impotent fury, leaps and spins in the stage center, her retinue dance wildly around her.

The dance of Fairy Carabosse in the scene with Princess Aurora is Grigorovich's wonderful innovation. The King and his courtiers bend over the lifeless Princess in horror and grief. Fairy Carabosse, disguised as a nun robed in black with a white piece on her head, appears among them and expresses her sympathy hypocritically.

Then she calmly moves backstage, her look proud and confident as though she has done her duty, where she throws her robes away, ridicules the crowd gloatingly, runs down the stairs, leans on her crutch and cursing all and everyone, vanishes out of sight through a hatch in the floor.

Fairy Carabosse, who danced in the half-bent pose of a decrepit old woman, suddenly straightens up in this scene. Her proud erect posture affirming the act of evil-doing is more terrifying than the spiteful moves of her grotesque dance.

The image of Fairy Carabosse is brought to completion in the finale of the Second Act. While Princess Aurora is asleep, Fairy Carabosse reigns supreme in her castle. She is ensconced on the backs of her retinue as if on a throne. She vigilantly guards the Princess, pricking her ears at the slightest noise, and benevolently plays with her minions, while all is quiet.

Some of the dwarfs are her favorites. Now she gently presses the head of one of them to her bosom, stroking his hair like a child's. This caressing gesture and the tenderness of the ferocious witch are sinister. But her image now seems so much richer and more meaningful. The grandeur and scope it assumes in this production are reminiscent of the scenes of Dante's *Inferno* and Gustave Doré's illustrations. It is clear that Fairy Carabosse is dedicated to evil because of her satanic hatred of life, youth and beauty. The fact that she was forgotten when other guests were invited to attend the festival is not the cause of her fury but just a convenient pretext for venting it.

This brings to light another characteristic feature of Grigorovich's art. In the traditional classical ballets goodness enjoyed an unchallenged rule. The images of evil simply provided a motive for affirming the reign of goodness and had no independent significance.

That was also the case in Petipa's original of *The Sleeping Beauty*, although in Tchaikovsky's music the image of Fairy Carabosse is equal in significance to the image of the Lilac Fairy. This distinctive feature of the old classical ballets may be the reason why they seem somewhat naive to us today. Indeed, in the present epoch of great social upheavals, an artistically persuasive portrayal of the triumph of good over evil requires an awareness of the real significance and scope of evil.

As is known, this is precisely the motive for the profound interpretation of such images in Dmitri Shostakovich's symphonic conceptions. In this writer's opinion, the same tendency is manifest in a different way in Grigorovich's art as well. His innovation is probably not expressed anywhere as fully and vividly as in his expansion and magnification of the significance and scope of the images of evil (Severyan in *The Stone Flower*, Rothbart in *Swan Lake*, the Vizier in *The Legend of Love*).

Take, in addition, the creation by Grigorovich of images with a complex and contradictory inner world unfamiliar to the old ballets (The Hostess of the Copper Mountain, Mehmene Banu, Drosselmeier).

In the image of Fairy Carabosse these two lines seem to be blended into a common whole. The image has been magnified to the extent of a symbolic personification of all evil. At the same time, it has acquired a truly Shakespearean sophistication. In Grigorovich's new production Fairy Carabosse has nothing of the elementary straightforwardness of her earlier interpretation but is remarkable for her satanically rich spiritual world.

The principle of magnifying the symbolic images of the fairies in *The Sleeping Beauty* can be traced back to the past productions. In Petipa's choreography the fairies had a purely "auxiliary" significance in relation to the images of the main heroes. In his production of 1922 Fedor Lopukhov developed the dance part of the Lilac Fairy, in particular, by inventing the brilliant "portrait" variation in the Prologue, which has become part and parcel of the canonized choreographic text along with Petipa's finest episodes.

Choreographers made repeated attempts to magnify the image of Fairy Carabosse, which became comparable to the part of the Lilac Fairy in choreographic vividness after the latter's enrichment by Lopukhov. These attempts, which are exemplified by K. Sergeyev's screen version of *The Sleeping Beauty* and by Yuri Grigorovich's preceding theatrical version, however, failed to have any spectacular results.

Success was achieved only in Grigorovich's new production of *The Sleeping Beauty*, which has influenced the entire structure of its imagery. First, Fairy Carabosse and Fairy Lilac have now been granted equal rights not only in the meaning of their parts but also choreographically, that is, in the artistic vividness of dance.

Second, these images have lost their "auxiliary" role in the development of the story and have assumed independent significance on a par with the images of Princess Aurora and Prince Desire. Thereby the accent of the ballet was transferred from the individual destinies of the young heroes to the common destiny of the world as embodied in the images of the two warring fairies.

Therefore, the moral message of the ballet has assumed a new dimension and been transformed from a lyrical into a "cosmic" global message. As a result, the ballet has lost its naiveté. Not only has it acquired a modern conception of evil but, what is most important, the significance and implication of the triumph of good over evil have increased immeasurably. All these factors account for the congeniality of the ballet with Tchaikovsky's music.

The matter, however, is not confined to this alone. The change in the scope and functions of the images personifying the main antagonism of the world demanded greater development of the parts of the young heroes. In Petipa's production Princess Aurora was the main character. That was consistent with the aesthetic principles of the old classical ballets, which were invariably female ballets. In them the female image played the leading role, while the male performed the duty of a "cavalier" and his part was for the most part reduced to supporting his female partner.

That was so in Petipa's *The Sleeping Beauty* where the dancer of the part of Prince Desire was to perform only a variation and a coda in *pas de deux*, while the rest of his part consisted of supports and pantomime.

Grigorovich has left the classically perfect image of Princess Aurora absolutely intact. However, he has imaginatively developed the part of Prince Desire and made it comparable in sophistication to the image of Princess Aurora. In his first production of *The Sleeping Beauty* the choreographer renounced the scene of the picnic so important for portraying the image of Prince Desire. He revived Petipa's original conception and restored the mimic characters of this scene: the tutor of Prince Desire and a Princess who was courted by him before he learned about Princess Aurora.

This in itself lent salient features to the image of Prince Desire and made it more life-like. However, the parts of the tutor and the Prince's lady friend in the ballet are not exclusively mimical ones. They are also expressed in dance. These characters, danced by coryphées, take part in the dances at the picnic. What matters most, of course, is the change in the character of the part of Prince Desire and the reinforcement of its dance elements, which has lent a new dimension to his image and made it a developing rather than static one. In the Second Act where the Prince makes his appearance for the first time Grigorovich has given Prince Desire three contrastive variations based on the choreography outlined by Petipa.

The first — entrée — variation is full of jubilation. The Prince literally flies out to the stage by soaring leaps. His dance is cheerful and conveys his ecstatic admiration for the beauty of the world and his enjoyment of youth. He also takes part, although briefly, in the common dances of the courtiers. He is still mingling with the crowd. After some time, however, he will refuse to join the merry company and remain alone, his mind absorbed in exalted dreams and vague desires.

In this scene Grigorovich has given him another, romantic, variation, which is reminiscent, in image content rather than in choreography, of Siegfried's variation in the First Act of *Swan Lake*. The theme of vague love dreams is further developed in the duet of Prince Desire with Fairy Lilac.

When Princess Aurora and the nereids make their appearance — in a scene choreographed after Petipa — the Prince takes part in a common dance ensemble (trio of Princess Aurora, Fairy Lilac and Prince Desire with a corps de ballet). This episode is called *pas d'action* (action dance) in the score.

The action here consists of these events: obeying Fairy Lilac, the nereids now bring Aurora and Desire closer to each other, now separate them, and the duet of the heroes reveals all the nuances of their mutual attraction and timid but growing love emotions. The episode as a whole forms a complex and well-developed polyphonic dance ensemble of a lyrical character — the culmination in conveying the romantic message of the ballet, including the appealing images of Princess Aurora and Prince Desire.

The beautiful phantom, however, vanishes out of sight. The new, third, variation of Prince Desire choreographed by Grigorovich expresses his supplication addressed to the Lilac Fairy and his impatience to see Princess Aurora again.

In the final act Prince Desire appears as a handsome young hero of remarkable spiritual and physical prowess, radiating strength and happiness. The duet of Aurora and Desire is so inspired and reveals such consummate beauty that the whole conflict situation of the ballet appears artistically warranted and conclusive: indeed, the triumph of goodness in the Universe is necessary for such perfect beauty of Man to flourish in freedom. The philosophical idea of the ballet is brought to its culmination here.

The more significant an idea, however, the greater the significance of the concrete fabric of a performance for its expression. Therefore, having deepened and sharpened the central images, Grigorovich was certainly bound to deal with their background. In this production he has invented the character dances (with the exception of the "fairy-tales") and whatever is linked with the characters of the royal court.

The dances of the courtiers in the opening scenes are merry but stiff; they are carefree and playful at the picnic, solemn and stately in the polonaise and the coda of the final act. The peasant farandole in the scene of the picnic contrasts in its naive simplicity with the exquisite and affected dances of the aristocrats. The dance of the knitting maidens at the beginning of the First Act full of humor, mischief and coquetry is especially fascinating.

Two trends typical of Grigorovich's art are appreciable in the choreography of the character genre scenes. He has by no means discarded pantomime but seeks to present all episodes as much in the language of dance as possible. This refers in particular to the aforementioned scene of the knitting maidens, which was based on pantomime in Petipa's production, whereas here it is a merry and picturesque dance which only enhances the story.

This also refers to the part of Cattalabutte, which has been supplemented with individual dance elements. Finally, this refers to reinforcing the part of the corps de ballet in some mass scenes (in the Prologue the choreographer has developed the male parts of the retinue of Fairy Carabosse, introduced a few "exclamations" of the corps de ballet in the adagio of Princess Aurora with four cavaliers, etc.).

Another trend is the enlargement of dance scenes by integrating a few musical numbers into a common extended number. Grigorovich very often resorts to this technique. The most striking example of that is the final act of *The Nutcracker* where all the music beginning from the waltz is embraced by a common choreographic scene. There are few reasons for that in *The Sleeping Beauty*. In one scene, however, this method proved indispensable. The choreographer renounced the fragmentation of dances at the picnic and integrated them into a complete divertissement scene, to which the peasant farandole stands out in sharp contrast.

In view of the tendency to enlarge choreographic scenes it would be relevant to mention another local but symptomatic solution in the scene of Princess Aurora with four cavaliers. The musical structure of this scene sets the form of *grand pas*: the introduction is followed by a majestic adagio and then by a variation, which is marked in the score as the variation of the Maids of Honor and pages.

In his earlier production of *The Sleeping Beauty* Grigorovich, applying his method of enlargement, entrusted the first variation to the four cavaliers, thereby converting this scene into what may be called a pure, model *grand pas.*

In his new production Grigorovich abandoned that, although the solution he had found earlier seemed to accord with the spirit of all his art. He returned the first variation to the children taking part in the corps de ballet. He was not motivated either by adulation of Petipa, or only by a desire to give the dancer of the part of Princess Aurora a respite before her difficult and responsible variation.

What matters most is that now the cavaliers no longer "eclipse" Princess Aurora, which was evident to some extent in the preceding production, because they are no longer her equal partners in the scene. Here they are simply her escorts, and the scene remains Princess Aurora's "portrait."

In this production this solution is of fundamental significance. In Grigorovich's choreography every act has assumed what may be called a representative "portrait" character. The Prologue is devoted to the images of the two fairies, the First Act to Princess Aurora, the Second Act to Prince Desire, and the Third Act to the triumph of the young heroes. This makes the production exceptionally clear-cut structurally and logical compositionally. In this production the dramaturgical law discussed above is completely revealed in the choreography.

The uniformity of each act established in Tchaikovsky's musical dramaturgy determines the structural logic of its stage composition. The initial scenes are in pantomime character style, every act is completed by a static composition. Between the introductory scene and the action finale there are two large dance scenes: divertissement (with predominance of character dance) and lyrical (classical ensemble). This regularity never transforms into a scheme anywhere but helps bring out the dramaturgical logic of the ballet.

As with any significant production *The Sleeping Beauty* in Grigorovich's choreography brought to prominence a brilliant constellation of dancers: Natalya Bessmertnova, Yekaterina Maximova, N. Semizorova, Lyudmila Semenyaka, Nadezhda Pavlova, I. Pyatkina, and N. Anianashvili in the part of Princess Aurora; V. Vasilyev, A. Bogaryrev, V. Gordeyev, A. Fadeyechev, N. Fedorov, and M. Liepa in the part of Prince Desire; V. Levashov, Y. Vetrov, Anatoly Simachev, and S. Radchenko in the part of Fairy Carabosse; Marina Leonova, Tatyana Golikova and other dancers of the part of the Lilac Fairy.

For all of them *The Sleeping Beauty* is a milestone in their artistic careers, revealing their talent and reinforcing their skill. In fact, this ballet has raised them to the pinnacles of artistry in the performing arts and polished their technique of classical dance.

Ballet Master's and Artist's Teamwork

The consummate perfection of the stage scenery of Grigorovich's version of *The Sleeping Beauty* deserves its own story. It is the work of one of the most brilliant stage designers and indisputably the best ballet scenographer Simon Bagratovich Virsaladze (b. 1909), who has been Grigorovich's permanent collaborator ever since the latter produced *The Stone Flower*. He has designed all of Grigorovich's ballets and greatly contributed to their spectacular success.

To understand and duly appreciate the significance of Virsaladze's art in Grigorovich's ballets, *The Sleeping Beauty* in particular, it would be relevant to describe some specific features and conditions of the artistic design of a ballet production, since Virsaladze is a past master in this area of artistic creativity.

The design of a ballet has its own specifics dictated by the genre of dance. It is more directly linked with the music than in opera, because the absence of a verbal text makes it incumbent on the artist to rely exclusively on the musical dramaturgy.

The synthesis of imitative art and music can be achieved only through choreographic action, whose different aspects are expressed by these arts. Thus, to ensure full accord with the message of the music, the stage design should be organically linked with the choreography.

But what does this mean in practical terms? What are the specific conditions of an artist's work dictated by the specifics of ballet? Indeed, a simultaneous perception of the design and dance does not necessarily imply their synthesis. Therefore, to blend with choreography into an organic common whole the design itself should have definite characteristics. What are they?

It is common knowledge that the conditions of the dance action dictate the need to free the stage for choreographic compositions. Therefore, complex sets with numerous props and elaborate decorations are much less common in ballet than in drama or opera. In the artistic design of ballet decor the emphasis is placed mainly on the backdrop, side-scenes, and the portal ornamentation of the stage.

Similarly, in designing costumes the ballet artist cannot confine himself to identifying the historical, social, ethnic and individual traits of a character. He is obliged to make costumes light and convenient for dance, emphasizing body lines and dance movements. The basis for the ballet costume, therefore, is a dance "uniform" which is imaginatively designed to fit the characters and content of a production.

The costumes of the main heroes are usually designed with greater attention to their individuality. The members of the corps de ballet are usually dressed identically, the costumes of different groups sometimes differing in design, with the exception of scenes of a large crowd. Take, for instance, the First Act of *Don Quixote* designed by Konstantin Korovin and the folk dances in *Romeo and Juliet* in the scenography of Pyotr Vilyams.

Identical costumes in a mass dance (for instance, in the dances of the "wilis", swans and nereids of classical ballets or Catherine's maiden friends in *The Stone Flower*, Mehmene Banu's "thoughts" in *The Legend of Love*) emphasize its emotional and symbolic significance and conform to the unity and generalization of a dance composition. In designing the costumes of individual characters, the ballet artist seeks to achieve a fusion of characteristic imitative styles of dress and dance.

All these are important but more or less "external" demands made by choreography on the artist's imagination. He is also confronted by the far more complicated and profound problem of adapting his design conception to the specific features of choreographic imagery: the musicality and symphony of dance action, its stylized generalization, emotionality and lyricism and, often, metaphorical significance.

Thus, the naturalness and realism of the stage scenery and costumes may be incongruous with the conventionalism of choreographic action, and conversely, an abstract and schematic decor may contradict a full-blooded emotional and psychologically true-to-life choreography.

The ballet artist seeks to express in the decor the idea content of a ballet, to design the environment and external aspect of the action in forms conforming to the figurative imagery of choreography. This secures the artistic integrity of a production, in which the conception of design unites the dramaturgy, the music and the choreography in a common whole.

The art of Simon Virsaladze is of classical significance in this field. Profoundly specific and organic for ballet, however, his art has nothing in common with sham innovation, something that is often in evidence in the art of scenographers trying to impress the audience at all costs. Virsaladze solves the most intricate problems of art, embodying the progressive trends in its development.

In his scenographic works, Virsaladze readily reckons with such natural requirements of choreography as making the stage free for dance compositions or designing light and comfortable costumes for dance. However, the essence of his art never boils down to this alone. It meets not only the "external" but also the "inner" requirements of choreography, creating a visible image which becomes the artistic epitome of a ballet, embodying the symphonic principle inherent in the music and the choreography, and finally, presenting a generalized and emotionally vivid artistic image.

Ballets designed by Virsaladze blend in an integral unity of imagery different components of an artistic idea constant for the whole performance but varying from act to act. This constant idea embodies the "kernel" of the imagery linked with the idea content of the ballet as a whole and has a figurative, symbolic and metaphorical significance. Such are the malachite casket in *The Stone Flower*, the screen reminiscent of an ancient Oriental legend in *The Legend of Love*, the hoary walls of gray stone in *Spartacus*, and the Russian church belfry in *Ivan the Terrible*, to take but a few examples.

The variable components of the stage scenery, which are usually painted backdrops, present scene-to-scene settings of the action.

In such stage design the general blends with the specific in a continuous succession of scenes, depicting with consummate mastery the characteristic events of musical and choreographic development.

Virsaladze has an unsurpassed sense of color: his scenic decoration invariably presents an elaborate yet subtle gamut of colors suggested by the character of the music and contributing substantially to sustaining the emotional atmosphere of the action. This color range is supplemented with an arrangement of light effects also planned to develop the music and action, as well as with the costumes color-coordinated with the decor and lending it greater power.

The light effects and costumes form the moving variable aspect of the stage scenery. In the development of the action they merge with the scenery into a common picturesque whole, and the stage seems to be filled with the rhythms of music and dance, presenting what may be called "a symphony in color."

Costumes designed by Virsaladze are meant to reveal and emphasize the beauty and character of dance by their style and color range. The artist skilfully combines the style of dance "uniform" with elements of an authentic real-life costume.

Virsaladze has a unique feeling for the specifics of a ballet performance. Freeing the stage for dance, he applies a few terse and bold strokes to revive on stage the atmosphere of an epoch and to make one appreciate the historical milieu. He never degrades the scenery to flat painted backdrops but combines them with a spatial decor design.

Virsaladze is a veritable magician of theatrical decor and an unexcelled designer of the ballet costume. His decor is airy and romantic, of very subtle colors, amazingly consonant with the music and the atmosphere of the story and ballet imagery.

Virsaladze invariably designs his costumes in keeping with the requirements of the choreography, and their cut and color add emphasis to dance movements. They combine organically with the stage scenery, developing and supplementing its artistic theme. Thanks to this unity the whole system of decor including the elaborate patterns of light effects seems to come to life, becomes mobile, as it were, and responds to the rhythms of the music. This is why Virsaladze's design is so often called "a symphony in color." Its consummate harmony makes it a perfect match for Grigorovich's choreography, which is a "symphony in dance."

Like Grigorovich, Virsaladze did not come up with brilliant artistic solutions for *The Sleeping Beauty* overnight. In fact, his production of 1973 had been preceded by another two versions.

Resuming his work on the decor of *The Sleeping Beauty* roughly once in every ten years (in 1952, 1963, and 1973), however, the artist never repeated his earlier solutions. Every new idea was consistent not only with his own evolution but also with the general progress of the Soviet art of scenic decoration.

Only one aspect of his art remained unchanged: the exceptional beauty, subtle taste and unexcelled mastery of the ballet costume.

In K. Sergeyev's production of 1952 at the Kirov Theater of Leningrad, there were ornate and gaily colored forms of baroque architecture and realistic park scenery on the stage, which were consonant with the festiveness of Tchaikovsky's music but slightly dissonant with its romantic message and fairy tale imagery.

In Yuri Grigorovich's version of *The Sleeping Beauty* staged at the Bolshoi in 1963 Virsaladze made the scenic decoration weightless and airy and dazzlingly white. The stage was dressed in snow-white tulle with fragmentary symbolic images painted in bold strokes to indicate the place of the action.

That decor was fantastically beautiful in its coloristic effects but in *The Sleeping Beauty* it was probably too "sterile" to fit its rich emotions and full-blooded life.

In the decor of the 1973 production Virsaladze disposed of the flaws of his earlier artistic solutions. His scenery here is just as airy and weightless (their main technique is picturesque appliqué on tulle) but they are highly imitative and descriptive. The images are concrete, it is true, but these are fantastic images from fairy tales. It is a world of romantic legends, ancient folk tales and reminiscences.

It is well-known that Grigorovich produced his version of *The Sleeping Beauty* in 1973 not as a fairy tale for children or as mere entertainment, as other choreographers had often done, but as a philosophical poem of its own kind, containing a profound conception and conveying a moral idea consistent with Tchaikovsky's music.

In that production he sharpened the conflict between good and evil and raised it to the level of a conflict between world forces, which lent a new dimension to the images of the main heroes. Virsaladze's decor is consonant with this serious theme and the significance of its general interpretation. His scenery is fantastically beautiful, as well as restrained and austere in tone. Their emotional and expressive colors never became gaudy in frantic pursuit of spectacular effects.

In the coloristic design of the decor, just as in other works of Virsaladze, the "achromatic tricolor" of black, gray and white has a great part to play. This is the basis on which the dominant color range is superimposed, which is different in every act. Gray and black predominate but they acquire numerous shades on exposure to color illumination.

The general tone of Virsaladze's decor is a smoky pearl color at places iridescent like mother-of-pearl. It is moving and unsteady and full of imperceptible shades and nuances. In every act this general background is dominated by a definite color range consistent with its emotional atmosphere and the character of events.

In the Prologue (festival at the palace celebrating Princess Aurora's birth) it is blue, in the First Act (park in front of the castle) it is greenish, in the Second Act (autumn forest) it is pinkish-red, in the Third Act (palace of joy and happiness) it is lilac with green. In addition, lilac is mingled into details of decor, costumes, and properties and is the leitmotif of all acts of the production. It is the color of the Lilac Fairy, the chief guardian angel of goodness.

The elaborate arrangement of light effects has a substantial role to play in the coloristic development of the action. The performance begins in darkness, then floodlights are focussed upon individual characters, which is followed by a gradual increase in general illumination. It seems as if every act is better lighted than the preceding one. The performance ends in radiant joy.

The spectator accustomed to the predominance of white in the earlier version may find an abundance of black and gray colors strange. This, however, will be true only at first glance. The black-gray background emphasizes the dramatic side of the story (in the Prologue the festival is at its height, while tragedy seems to lurk in the corners of the castle) and forms amazingly beautiful combinations with the color range of every act.

A special role in the decor of *The Sleeping Beauty* is played by the panorama where the stage scenery stays alone with the music, and the artist has an opportunity to bring his brilliant talent and superior skill into full play. In Virsaladze's first stage setting the panorama was green and in the second it was conventional white. Now all of it is based on black and silvery colors with added red and pink illumination but the real-life character of the scenery is preserved.

The Lilac Fairy and Prince Desire sail in a boat to Princess Aurora's castle across smooth waters surrounded by a fairy tale forest. In the scene of this forest Virsaladze has achieved an amazing ornamental variety and wealth of decorative forms with very bold colors. This panorama has its denser and pale parts, its own culminations and rhythms. The stage is flooded with what seems to be "visible music" in the literal sense. It is just as charming as Tchaikovsky's melody flowing on the background of a measured accompaniment and just as mysterious as the romantic calls and intonations of the orchestra.

Virsaladze has achieved virtuoso mastery in designing costumes. The real and fantastic worlds in *The Sleeping Beauty* differ outwardly primarily in costumes, which are in genre "character style" in the former and in symbolic "dance style" in the latter. All costumes, however, are related to decor in color. They either develop its coloristic "theme" or supplement it with new colors and elements.

As part of the dance, the costumes lend a dynamic rhythm to imitative interpretation consonant with the rhythms of the music and contributing to integrating sight and sound impressions into a common whole. The supreme manifestation of this synthesis is perhaps the costumes of the waltz forming with the decor and the music an amazingly integral and harmonious accord (here numerous hues of pale green and golden brown are presented in combination with white).

The costumes of the heroes correspond to their characters and roles in the development of the story and their emotional states. The costume of Princess Aurora at the time of her childhood is pink and reminiscent of the color of dawn as her name suggests while at the time of her youth it is snow-white. The costume of Prince Desire is golden-brown with a scarlet cloak or dazzling white. The costume of the good Lilac Fairy corresponds to her name and that of the evil Fairy Carabosse is black and gold, and her hair is flaming red.

The costumes contain many amazing details. For instance, Virsaladze has designed with the utmost exquisiteness the female waltz costume with an oblique green appliqué on a snow-white skirt. This cut seems to be in perfect harmony with the main movement (balancé) in the choreography of the waltz. The artist has ingeniously expressed the class distinctions between the dances of the courtiers and the peasants at the picnic by the structural complexity of the costumes of the aristocracy and the simple clothes of the common folk.

One needs a highly developed sense of color to subdue so expertly the scarlet color of the cloaks and mantles of the courtiers in the final act in order to harmonize it with the other, silvery parts of their clothes.

Seeing this harmonious system of decor and costumes in motion conforming to the flow, rhythms and dynamic variations of the music, one thinks of human genius that has created this triple symphony in color, music, and dance.

SYNOPSIS
THE SLEEPING BEAUTY

The ceremony of christening the baby girl born to King Florestan XIV is attended by all the good fairies led by The Lilac Fairy. They present their gifts to the Princess, named Aurora, and endow her with fine human character traits.

Unfortunately, the Master of Ceremonies, Cattalabutte, forgets to invite the evil Fairy Carabosse to attend the festival. Driven to frenzy by this show of disrespect, Fairy Carabosse comes to the festival as an ugly old witch with a retinue of bats and rats. She puts a curse on the Princess and predicts her death from injury with a spindle on reaching maidenhood.

Though Fairy Lilac is unable to break the curse, she can mitigate it with her magic power. Princess Aurora is to be put to a century-long sleep which will last until she is awakened by the kiss of a handsome Prince.

The day when the Princess is to come of age draws nearer. The King issues a decree banning possession in his kingdom of any sharp object that could injure the Princess. When some maidens are discovered to be using knitting needles, the King becomes infuriated. Unwilling to spoil the festival, however, he pardons the culprits, and all guests abandon themselves to merriment. At the height of the festival Fairy Carabosse appears in disguise and gives the Princess the present of a spindle. Playing with it carelessly, the Princess suddenly injures her finger and faints away. Thus, the prediction of the evil witch comes true. Fairy Lilac saves Princess Aurora from death by putting her to sleep along with all the residents of the castle. The dormant castle becomes overgrown with a thick forest.

One hundred years pass. Hunting game in a forest, Prince Desire, aided by Fairy Lilac, finds his way to the dormant kingdom, enters the castle and awakens the Princess from her eternal sleep with a kiss. Their love destroys the evil spell of Fairy Carabosse.

Distinguished guests assemble for the wedding of Princess Aurora and Prince Desire. The fairies and characters from Perrault's fairy-tales are among them (Big Bad Wolf, Little Red Riding Hood, Puss 'n Boots, Princess Florina, Blue Bird, and many others). It is the final triumph of love, goodness and beauty. This is the apotheosis of the ballet.

In the palace of King Florestan XIV, a huge christening party is taking place. Attending the feast are all the good fairies, including the most powerful fairy of them all, the Lilac Fairy. The new princess is christened Princess Aurora.

As it should be in a fairy tale, all the fairies have names which designate human characteristics. Thus we find the most popular fairies are the Fairy of Generosity, the Fairy of Carefreeness, the Fairy of Bravery, and so forth. All of these magnificently costumed fairies dance together, seemingly very happy that the beautiful new Princess Aurora will be the center of attraction in the palace of King Florestan XIV. Amidst all of these beautiful fairies is the fairy leader, the Lilac Fairy.

The Lilac Fairy is the most powerful of all the good fairies. She advises the other fairies on proper behavior and, in the case of the birth of Princess Aurora, she has given a sign to each good fairy to bestow admirable qualities upon the newborn Princess. The Lilac Fairy almost always wears a lilac-colored costume and she can always be seen in a prominent position when dancing with the other fairies.

The Fairy of Generosity dances in utter happiness as she bestows her blessings on the newborn Princess.

The Fairy of Carefreeness presents the new Princess Aurora with an easy-going spirit.

The Fairy of Bravery
endows the Princess
with self–
assuredness.

After each fairy, with delicate little wings attached to the back of her costume, presents her gift of good traits, they all dance together. The dance is light and joyful as you would expect from these wonderful fairies who might even be called "Angels."

As the dance continues the Lilac Fairy emerges from the background and assumes her position as the most powerful of all fairies. She is lifted into the air as she bestows her own secret blessings upon Princess Aurora.

Suddenly, without warning, disaster looms in the presence of the most powerful of all evil fairies, Fairy Carabosse. Fairy Carabosse is furious that she was not invited to the christening, and in a rage she predicts death to the Princess Aurora from a spindle, when the Princess reaches maidenhood. The good fairies beg Fairy Carabosse to remove her curse, but without success.

n the Lilac Fairy appears and fights the spell of Fairy Cara-
se. Being unable to lift the curse, she is able to change it
n death to a long sleep which can only be lifted when she
issed by a handsome Prince. She then chases the Fairy Cara-
se away.

It is now 16 years later. Princess Aurora has become a palace favorite, everyone loves her, and this is now a birthday party celebrating her sixteenth birthday. All the little children of the noblemen attached to the Palace attend the party. They are all dancing and holding garlands of flowers.

The dance continues with little girls and boys holding baskets
and showing off their fineries. This is a charming dance scene
where young people dance with grace and precision.

Suddenly the boys disappear and the girls perform a delightfully charming dance which is, at the same time, playful, graceful and extremely elegant.

The boys come back to dance with the girls and, holding them gently around their waists, show tender loving admiration for their partners. This is a magnificent display of dancing ability by young people.

Then, quite suddenly, the greeting dance is over and the Master of Ceremonies announces the imminent arrival of Princess Aurora who will, on this day, select her future husband.

Princess Aurora appears in her pretty pink costume. Full of life and happy as can be! She elegantly comes down the stairs.

How happy Princess Aurora is as she dances all around, full of life, greeting all her guests with a charming smile.

Naturally, Princess Aurora is admired by all the available Princes in attendance and they dance with her. The four princes, each in love with Aurora, tell her of their love and devotion. Aurora listens carefully to each of her lovers' promises.

Her happiness is
boundless as she
reaches for the
heavens supported
by her loyal
admirers.

As she dances all around the stage, she becomes attracted to a kindly old lady. Closer and closer she dances to the lady until finally she accepts the birthday gift offered to her. It is a spindle used in weaving.

As soon as she touches it, the beautiful Princess Aurora falls down in a death-like sleep. Her guests are in shock as the four princes rush to her aid . . . and the old lady comes forward to center stage.

With a fiendish gesture, she flings aside her modest cloak and reveals that she is not a kindly old lady at all, but is none other than the wicked Fairy Carabosse whose dreadful prophesy has come true.

But all is not lost! Suddenly the Lilac Fairy appears and everybody begins to hope that she can lift the dreadful curse of Fairy Carabosse. To save Aurora she puts everyone to sleep, thus the legend of the dormant kingdom begins.

The scene shifts to another palace 100 years later. A party is taking place. The Ladies of the palace of Prince Desire are dancing while their men are at a hunting party. Even the peasants are attracted by the music and perform folkdances for the amusement of the Ladies of the court.

Like an arrow shot into the air, Prince Desire arrives.

He flies like a bird and is the most handsome Prince in the kingdom. His skill as a dancer is legendary.

But something is missing in Prince Desire's happiness. He seems to be reaching for something that isn't there. He is left alone.

Suddenly the Lilac Fairy appears and he bows on his knee before her. "Follow me" she seems to indicate.

Suddenly, without warning, a
large group of wood nymphs
appear right before the Prince's
eyes. How wonderful and
powerful is Lilac Fairy.

Suddenly, without warning, a
magnificent nymph arises in the
vision of the Prince. It is Aurora
and Prince Desire hastens to
her.

The Prince touches her gently . . . he can hardly believe she is real.

The fantasy continues as the Prince tries to understand what is happening in his fantasy.

The Prince boldly lifts Aurora in his arms vowing never to let her go . . . then Aurora disappears.

The Prince searches for Princess Aurora and stumbles upon the sleeping kingdom. He still isn't sure that his dream was not a reality . . . until he sees Princess Aurora in a deep sleep. His kiss awakens Princess Aurora and he proposes that they be married in a great royal wedding feast. (Facing page): The wedding party begins with all the heroes of fairy tales attending. The theme of the party is "good and evil." The first guests to arrive are the famous Puss 'n' Boots and his girlfriend, the White Pussycat.

First Puss 'n' Boots has a fight with his girlfriend, the White Pussycat.

Then they settle their problems and cuddle.

Princess Florine
and the Bluebird
of Happiness
come to
congratulate the
bride and groom.

Princess Florine listens intently to the tender call of this sweet-voiced Bluebird of Happiness. She quickly becomes quite happy under the spell of his charming song.

The Bluebird of
Happiness flies
through the air in
a ritual of love.

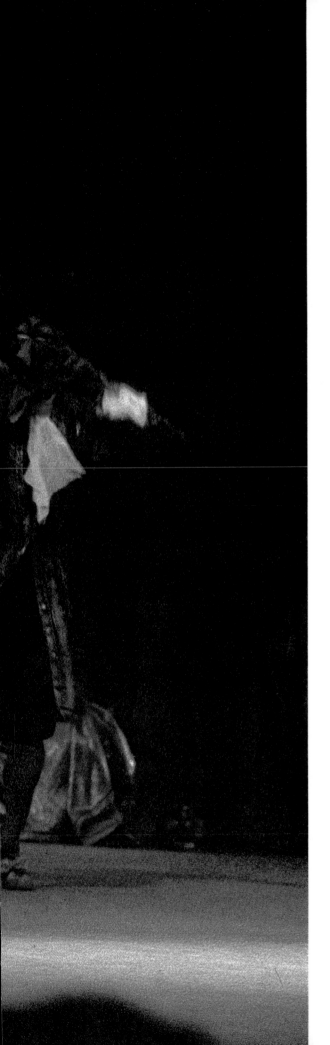

Quite suddenly another
guest rushes into the
scene. It is no one less
familiar than Little Red
Riding Hood being
chased by the ever-
hungry Wolf trying to
catch her and eat her!
But Little Red Riding
Hood cries out for help
. . . and she is saved.
Another example of
good and evil!

The duet of Cinderella and Prince Fortune merges into a scene of mutual love. It is a glorious dance. What a wonderful party for Princess Aurora and Prince Desire!! All the famous stars of fairy tales are there. These same fairy tales are known all around the world as are the stars of these fairy tales . . . in which Justice always triumphs over evil . . . beauty over ugliness . . . and goodness over badness.

The Fairy of Diamonds entertains the royal couple with her magnificent dance in which her costume sparkles with diamonds.

Finally the royal pair dance.

. . . and dance.

How elegant and royal are the Prince and Princess *(see also the facing page)*.

Their dancing becomes the highlight of the ballet as the Prince and Princess *(see also facing page)* express their love with dances of the utmost skill.

Prince Desire reiterates his vows of love and devotion *(above)* while Princess Aurora relates how happy she is that Prince Desire found her and awakened her from her 100 year long sleep *(facing page)*.

The dance of the royal pair continues with more variations portraying their great love and happiness *(facing page)*.

The magnificent Natalya Bessmertnova, the prima ballerina of the Bolshoi, made ballet history with her performance as Princess Aurora.

Conclusion

The Sleeping Beauty of Tchaikovsky in Petipa's choreography is one of the finest specimens of ballet. But ballet is not a museum and its productions are not exhibits that remain unchanged indefinitely. They have an historical life of their own. Every generation and every epoch make their own demands upon them, see them in a different light, and give them their own distinctive interpretation.

In the course of their history ballet productions often grow old and lose their vigor and inspiration, while some of them, which at one time were extremely popular, sink into oblivion without a trace.

Often the original choreography of a ballet is revised and supplemented, so much so that its text, very much admired at birth, is totally forgotten or distorted.

It may happen, however, that a ballet is reborn, as it were. It is given a new lease on life, and its inherent artistic potentials, which lay dormant, are brought into play. Ballets capable of such revival live for centuries.

This holds true in full measure for *The Sleeping Beauty*. It is a work of genius in its very essence, and though that was perceptible at its birth, the ballet witnessed periods of rising and declining popularity with the public. During the 100 years of its life on stage the ballet repeatedly became old-fashioned and was revised; much of its excellence was lost but good traditions developed in its performance, and individual details and aspects were improved.

The Sleeping Beauty has known superficial interpretations, which left almost nothing of its profound message, and poor casts unable to measure up to the difficult tasks set by its choreography. It was at times converted into a "divertissement" or a fairy tale for children. Nor has it been spared the ravages of inept attempts to modernize it to the degree of absurdity.

But finally there came a day when its beauty and philosophy were revealed more forcefully than ever before, and its original choreography was advanced to a much higher artistic level without discarding any of its valuable components.

That wonderful event was Grigorovich's version of *The Sleeping Beauty* staged at the Bolshoi in 1973. In that production modern interpretations and imagery combined with classical heritage and creative development. The ballet was truly inspired, exciting and beautiful. Ballet-lovers the world over are invariably fascinated by it whenever they have a rare chance to see this masterpiece of music, dance and scenography.

The Waltz of the Flowers.

This ballet shows the most fruitful ways to follow in modern choreography. Dozens of brilliant dancers have reached the pinnacles of artistry and fame in this production. It is certainly destined to have a very long life, because its profound and lofty message of love and goodness, its consummate beauty and perfection arouse the noblest feelings in spectators, strengthen their faith in the eventual triumph of good over evil and elevate them spiritually.

LIST OF CHARACTERS AND DANCERS IN "THE SLEEPING BEAUTY"

Princess Aurora usually wears a pink costume before her 100 year long sleep, and a white costume after she meets Prince Desire.

When she appears with Prince Desire she wears a white costume.

Index

This scene depicts one of the four princes who are courting Princess Aurora before her fateful accident which resulted in her 100 year long sleep. Note the authentic and elaborate detailing of the costumes of the male dancers. This attention to detail in all respects is a distinguishing trait of Grigorovich productions.

Prince Desire holding Princess Aurora aloft before she disappears from his vision.